Essays on the Love Commandment

Essays
on the
Love Commandment

by

Luise Schottroff   Christoph Burchard
Reginald H. Fuller   M. Jack Suggs

Translated by

REGINALD H. and ILSE FULLER

FORTRESS PRESS   Philadelphia

The book is a translation of excerpts from *Jesus Christus in Historie und Theologie*, edited by Georg Strecker (c) 1975 by J. C. B. Mohr (Paul Siebeck), Tübingen, "The Antitheses as Redactional Products" by M. Jack Suggs having already appeared originally in English in that volume.

Library of Congress Cataloging in Publication Data

Main entry under title:

Essays on the love commandment.

Selections from a Festschrift honoring Hans Conzelmann published in Tübingen in 1975 under title: Jesus Christus in Historie und Theologie.
CONTENTS: Schottroff, L. Non-violence and the love of one's enemies.—Fuller, R. H. The double commandment of love.—Burchard, C. The theme of the Sermon on the Mount.—Suggs, M. J. The antitheses as redactional products.
1. Jesus Christ—Teachings—Addresses, essays, lectures. 2. Love (Theology)—Biblical teaching—Addresses, essays, lectures. 3. Conzelmann, Hans—Addresses, essays, lectures. I. Schottroff, Luise.
BS2417.L7J4713   241'.6'77   78-54550
ISBN 0-8006-0528-4

7124F78   Printed in the United States of America   1–528

Contents

Preface

The four essays in this volume were excerpted from a much larger volume entitled *Jesus Christus in Historie und Theologie,* edited by Georg Strecker as a *Festschrift* for Hans Conzelmann on the occasion of his sixtieth birthday (October 27, 1975).

The original volume was divided into two sections. The first section dealt with the problem of the historical Jesus and the kerygmatic Christ—that is, with the historical Jesus as reconstructed by the historical–critical method, and with the proclamation of the Christ event in the post–Easter community. From this section the essay by Luise Schottroff is taken, since it deals with the way in which the commandment of love for the enemy was taken up and understood in the proclamation of the Christian church after Easter.

The second section of the *Festschrift* was devoted to essays concerning the understanding of Christ and the proclamation "of" Christ—the genitive "of" being understood in both an objective and a subjective sense. The three essays, my own, that of Christoph Burchard, and that of M. J. Suggs come from this second section. My essay on the double commandment of love was included here because it dealt with an aspect of the proclamation of Christ (subjective genitive). In different ways, the Burchard and Suggs essays are concerned with the aspects of the evangelist Matthew's understanding of Christ. Several of the essays in the original volume originated as papers read at the international seminar on the question of the historical Jesus at the annual meetings of the SNTS

(Studiorum Novi Testamentum Societas) since 1969. The essays by Professor Suggs and myself were first presented in that context. Professor Schottroff also participated in this seminar, but chose to contribute a different paper to the *Festschrift*. All except Professor Suggs' contribution have been translated from the German.

These four essays were selected from the total of twenty-seven because they all relate in one way or another to the love commandment, or to the Sermon on the Mount as its quintessential expression. If the centrality of the love commandment rests, as my essay has tried to show, upon the authentic teaching of Jesus, its interpretation and application is a fresh task for every succeeding generation. The evangelist Matthew, writing toward the end of the first century, provided one of the most influential interpretations. For, as Professor Burchard frankly observes, the Sermon on the Mount is from Matthew, not from Jesus. And Matthew's purpose, as Professor Burchard concludes, was to define and exhibit the True Law, and to call men and women to discipleship in obedience to that Law. Professor Schottroff, in the course of her exploration into the most radical aspect of the love commandment—the love for the enemy—shows among other things how this commandment has been understood in our own century by Martin Luther King, who lived and died for that understanding. Perhaps even more important, she reminds us that any contemporary attempt to interpret and apply that law must take into account the power–relationships in any given society. In this way she brings sociological insights to bear upon the hermeneutical problem.

Much contemporary ethical discussion, while claiming to be Christian, has been conducted without reference to the biblical norms. There are signs of awareness both on the side of biblical scholarship and on the side of Christian ethics that this ought not to be, and attempts are being made to redress the situation. Let us hope that these essays may contribute something to those attempts.

REGINALD H. FULLER

LUISE SCHOTTROFF

Non-Violence and the Love of One's Enemies

Matthew 5:38–48 and Luke 6:27–36

THE MEANING OF LOVE
OF THE ENEMY

The command to love our enemies is often taken to be universal in its scope. It is understood to mean a general love of humanity "always and toward everybody."[1] The commandment to love our enemy is taken as an unlimited expansion of the commandment to love our neighbor. In this case, it does not much matter whether the enemy we are to love is our personal adversary or one from whom we differ in matters of faith. Yet it may be observed that in this interpretation the primary model for the love of our enemy is derived from the personal sphere, where the individual meets his own particular adversary. It is taken for granted that this model can be transferred to other spheres of life. All the interest is focused upon what happens to the person who does the loving. It will help us to grasp this wider understanding of the command if we see how Rudolf Bultmann and Herbert Braun interpret it. Each of these scholars, of course, has his own theological ideas. Yet what they say about love of the enemy remains basically within the framework we have just sketched out.

For R. Bultmann love of the enemy is "an overcoming of self-will in the concrete situation of life in which a person encounters another person."[2] The emphasis lies on the subject who loves, on his victory over self, not on the recipient of the love. The fact that

9

the object of love is an enemy is "the high point of overcoming self."[3] This is not love for humankind in general "based upon the idea of humanity" and concerned with the personal dignity of the subject or "the value of other persons."[4] Such an approach merely rules out certain reasons for the love of others but does not change the basic principle that any human being could be the other person we have to love. The practice of love (*"What a man must do"*) need not be taught. "It is assumed that everyone knows that."[5] Similarly the commandment to turn the other cheek rests quite naturally on the basic principle of the obedience the believer owes to God.[6] "As obedient to God, setting aside my selfish will, renouncing my own desires, I stand before my neighbor, prepared for sacrifice for neighbor as for God."[7] Here the theological interest is shifted to the believer in a way which contradicts the parenesis in Matt. 5:38ff. In it are given instructions for action,[8] and the objects of love, the enemies, are described in detail. But the most important objection to Bultmann's interpretation lies in the fact that self-love and the attitude of natural man are in no way the theme of the text. The "sinners" who only love those who also love them (Luke 6:32–34 par.) are not sinners in the sense of man in his natural egotism, of whom Bultmann speaks, but people who love their neighbors but not their enemies. Again, Bultmann's suggestion that the saying excludes any humanitarian thinking introduces a consideration completely absent from the texts in question, which have no inhibitions about using ideas from contemporary ethical systems.[9] Bultmann's definition of the commandment to love one's enemy introduces a theological interpretation which cannot be harmonized with Matt. 5:38ff. par.

Much of the same is true of Herbert Braun. His definition may be more representative than Bultmann's for the widespread interpretation of the commandment to love one's enemy in the context of general humanitarian love. His emphasis also lies on the subject who is to love. For Braun Jesus requires "love of the enemy, and thereby widens the idea of the neighbor to an unprecedented degree."[10] This extension of meaning is not intended as an abstract definition,[11] but as a matter of practical urgency.[12] In it Jesus comes in conflict with the "religious tradition of Judaism" and the Old

Testament,[13] though not as a matter of principle. The enemy is
one's personal as well as religious adversary.[14] This produces "a
relative, though not basic openness toward the non-Jewish neighbor."[15] True, there would seem to be a difference between Matt.
5:38ff. par. and an explicit command to love humanity in general.
But there is no difference about the circle of people to be loved.
The difference lies only in the way the command is formulated—
particularly in its urgency. This, however, is of theological significance. The urgency makes it impossible to evade the commandment by fulfilling it in a merely formal way. The point at issue
is not that a certain amount of love is required ("the left cheek,
the second mile, the coat"),[16] after which "self-defense would become permissible." No, the real meaning is that there should be a
"yes—without limit or measure."[17] The urgency, concreteness, and
radicalism of the commandment is an important barrier against all
casuistry and hair-splitting attempts at definition.[18] On the historical level Braun sees a particular type of Jewish piety under
attack. Theologically his interest is directed against present day
hair-splitting by the pious who evade the radical nature of the
commandment. The reason for this radical emphasis, the "yes—
without limit," is that otherwise the loving subject might display a
wrong attitude. Unfortunately, this interpretation is open, in principle at any rate, to the same objections as that of Bultmann. You
cannot deduce from this commandment (Matt. 5:38) a polemic
directed against a casuistic or merely formal obedience. After all,
the critique of the Old Testament and Judaism came in only at a
later stage in the tradition, viz., in Matthew's antitheses. Braun
makes the command to turn the other cheek a means of distinguish-
ing between the believer and the sinner. That is what makes his
position rather similar to Bultmann's, even though Braun does not
explicitly mention the sinner. The person who is bent on defending
himself against his enemy and on diluting the commandment by a
mere formal obedience is contrasted with the believer who practices
genuine obedience. The practice of love and its objects, i.e., the
enemy, are in no sense a matter for reflection, as is the case in
Matt. 5:38ff. par. Rather, Braun focuses his attention on the
individual and his inability to love. What Braun emphasizes is

the urgency of the commandment in contemporary application. And this sense of urgency helps to prevent a merely formal observance with a consequent evasion of its requirement. This interpretation misses the whole point of Matt. 5:38ff. In fact, it comes closer to certain other texts in the synoptic Gospels, for example, Luke 10:29.

We now turn to an alternative interpretation which no longer operates within the context of love of humanity, but rather takes the love of enemy as a concrete social event. Here love toward the enemy is a non-violent act of opposition on the part of Christians against the enemies of their faith and their overwhelming power. Such an interpretation is not interested in what goes on in the heart of the one who loves, but rather on its effect in the heart of the enemy.

Johannes Weiss' interpretation of the command to love one's enemy as an integral part of Jesus' eschatological preaching tends in this direction. It is not "the pathetic squabbles of day-to-day life which we survive more or less unruffled, that provide the battle-ground to prove our love for our enemies. . . . Only when we have to fight with our backs to the wall for the supreme values of life, for our faith and convictions, and deadly enmity comes our way, do we have the chance to show whether we are really capable of that spiritual freedom which Jesus expects of his disciples."[19]

In his commentary on Luke Heinz Schürmann has some striking illustrations of this kind of love for the enemies of our faith: "here is required that ultimate, creative goodness which makes all malice disappear . . . such love takes the evil to its heart and crushes it to death."[20] The most important exposition of our subject comes from Martin Luther King. The meaning of love [for the enemy] is not to be confused with some sentimental outpouring. It is a struggle in which the enemy is conquered without the use of military weapons and it enables the enemy to share in the benefits of the freedom we have won.[21] Love of the enemy means maintaining a posture of non-violent resistance in a "bloodless coup."[22] Part of the practice of loving our enemy means making a direct appeal to our "most relentless foe." "We shall match your capacity to inflict suffering by our capacity to endure suffering . . . Do to us what you will, and we shall continue to love you."[23] If the love of enemy is understood in this sense as a stance of combative resistance, it behooves us to define more closely the respected roles of enemy and combatant within the power structures of society. For in a case like this the love of enemy is an attitude adopted by groups which have no means of legal redress as the rest of society does. Thus the commandment is not regarded here as a universally applicable ethical rule[24] to be followed by everyone at any time. Rather, it is the attitude expected of Christians when they encounter resistance. It must always be distinguished from general humanitarian love and compassion, things which can be taught and practiced independently of the power structures of society. The strong can show love and compassion for the weak and *vice versa,* but love of the enemy is practiced by the weak toward the strong. Only those who are involved in resistance can teach this or demand it. Where it is recommended from the outside it becomes something totally different. It asks for the abandonment of resistance.[25]

This definition of love for the enemy can be verified without difficulty as an interpretation of Matt. 5:44ff. par. This passage is in fact speaking of the enmity between Christians and their persecutors. We may assume that in the early days of Christianity the Christians were socially at a disadvantage in this conflict. Whether intercessory prayer, blessing, and love can be regarded as constituent parts of the struggle against the enemies of the faith is something we shall need to examine. When the love of enemy is defined in this way, sociological investigation becomes a methodological necessity. The practitioners of love and their enemies in Matt. 5:44ff. par. cannot be viewed in abstraction from the social structures in which they live.

To be sure, this interpretation of the love of enemy as a way of overcoming opponents through love runs into difficulties when we examine the texts of the Jesus tradition. How is the prohibition of resistance in Matt. 5:39–41 to be understood? In interpretations like those of Bultmann and Braun the practitioner of love confronts his enemy without claiming anything from him. He says yes unconditionally to his enemy—he forgives him. The injunction to turn the other cheek illustrates this. It is an extreme instance of the renunciation of any claim. But when we love our enemies by over-coming evil with good we do not exactly accept them as they are. Such a love demands everything from them. It seeks to transform their enmity. Martin Luther King expresses himself in flat contradiction to Matt. 5:39 quite succinctly: "We cannot in all good conscience obey your unjust laws, because non-cooperation with evil is as much a moral obligation as is cooperation with good. Throw us into jail and we shall still love you."[26] Johannes Weiss sensed this contradiction between an active love of the enemy and the prohibition of resistance, but he was not able to solve the dilemma.[27] Nor does Heinz Schürmann offer any solution. Active love of the enemy[28] cannot be reconciled with the idea of a "love that does not react," as he attempts to do.[29] The problem remains unsolved—Why is resistance forbidden here, and alongside of it an active love for the enemy enjoined? What is the act of love meant to be if we are to offer the other cheek to our enemy? It only makes the injustice he inflicts so much the greater.

Martin Hengel and P. Hoffmann have put forward an interpretation of the command to love the enemy which helps us a step forward here. They take Matt. 5:38–48 as an attack on the Zealot position. Jesus—or, if you prefer, the Q community—is enjoining the "way of peaceableness,"[30] the "way of non-violence,"[31] and rejects the idea of violent rebellion against the Romans. With this interpretation it is possible to harmonize the prohibition of resistance with the injunction to love the enemy. It would be a prohibition against resorting to force of arms and that would by no means exclude an active love for the enemy. Thus it is logical that Hengel should regard Martin Luther King as an example of the "power of non-violence" which owes its inspiration to Jesus.[32] Unfortunately Matt. 5:30 cannot be regarded as an anti-Zealot text at any level of the tradition. The point at issue here is the enemies of the *Christians* and not the Romans as the enemies of the Jews. Though it may be true to say that the early Christians avoided the Zealot movements, this text does not enjoin the love of enemy as a way for Jews to deal with the hostility of Rome. The enemies of Christianity at this time were different from those who engaged the Zealots and were certainly not the agents of the Roman empire.[33] Among the enemies

who confronted the Christians we shall have to envisage various
ethnic groups, both Jewish and non-Jewish. We cannot assume that
the people who persecuted the Christians were the same as those
who persecuted the Jews, at least at no time after the persecution
of the Christians by Paul. That is the error of Hengel and Hoffmann.
If we want to take Matt. 5:38ff. as an anti-Zealot text, we shall
have to reconstruct a time in which the enemies of the Christians or
of the disciples of Jesus were not yet a problem. But even the historical Jesus himself could hardly have spoken of "enemies" or
"persecutors" without thinking of his own conflicts and those of his
disciples. There can be no question here of any direct opposition
to the Zealot movement. Yet Hengel and Hoffmann have a point.
The prohibition of resistance and the injunction to love the enemy
do have political implications. At this level the questions they ask
make sense. As for the sense in which political implications are involved, that is something we shall have to clarify later.

THE LOVE OF ENEMY
IN NON-CHRISTIAN ANTIQUITY

The themes of Matt. 5:38ff. par. were dealt with in antiquity
from time immemorial. We find them discussed almost every-
where—in ancient oriental parenesis, in the Old Testament, in
post-biblical Judaism, and in Greek and Roman literature.[34] It
goes without saying that the transmitters and recipients of early
Christian parenesis were alike acquainted with such ethical teachings inculcating a positive attitude towards the enemy and the
renunciation of retribution, the forgoing of revenge and anger.
The theme occurs not merely on a theoretical level in philosophical
literature but is applied directly to practical, everyday living
through proverbs and anecdotes. Thus it was not merely a topic for
discussion among the educated classes.

The relationship between the early Christian commandment of
love for the enemy and the ethical teachings of non-Christian
antiquity has frequently been discussed. Usually an attempt is made
to demonstrate the novelty and uniqueness of Jesus' commandment
in this regard.[35] Two objections can be raised against this method
of approach. First, it fails to do justice to the intentions of early

Christianity itself. When the command to love one's enemy is understood as an expression of the distinctively Christian life-style, in fact as something "new,"[36] then a line of demarcation with respect to the actual practice of love in society is drawn. But there is no intention of denying that comparable ethical injunctions also exist outside of Christianity. Such injunctions found in the Old Testament were appealed to by Christians.[37] And when from apologetic motives the love for the enemy was characterized as human kindness (*philanthrōpia*),[38] then attention was drawn to the connection between this Christian teaching and the ethical traditions of antiquity—even though this connection tends to blur the distinctiveness of early Christian teaching.

Second, the emphasis on differences brought to light by comparing ethical formulations and ideas and deducing from them differences in the content and substance of ethics is unsatisfactory. (Such an approach would, for instance, ask whether the other tradition was really speaking of *agapē* toward the enemy[39] and what serves as basis and rationale for the ethical attitude.[40]) The whole problem is left in an unsatisfactory state. If, for example, we agree with Nissen that the Old Testament and Judaism never speak of love for the enemy and that any such notion is excluded for theological reasons,[41] this would imply (or at least make it possible to infer) that Christianity is a superior religion to Judaism, however we choose to conceive that superiority. Such a comparison implies a scale of ethical or religious values so long as the differences on both sides are not described as historically or socially conditioned.[42]

The limitations imposed by historical factors can, in my opinion, only be grasped rightly in socio-historical categories. That is to say, we must look for the causes behind the differences. The renunciation of revenge by slaves against their masters is hardly comparable with the renunciation of revenge by kings against their defeated enemies (to mention two extreme cases), even if the ethical formula is verbally identical. By approaching the question in socio-historical terms we shall discover that even the non-Christian ethical discussion is fraught with internal discrepancies and exhibits contradictory attitudes. In what follows we shall try to differentiate between such attitudes. It may help to illuminate the distinctive character of early Christian ethical teaching and practice. It may also perhaps be helpful in enabling us to identify Christian practice today. What we need to know in the field of ethics is where the acting subject in question and its object are to be found in their social context. Ethical thinkers in the ancient world were much clearer about this question than we usually are today. Seneca, for instance, sees the problem clearly: "A contest with one's equal is hazardous, with a superior mad, with an inferior degrading."[43] I have chosen three different attitudes of renunciation of revenge to illustrate such differentiations.

a) *The Underdog—A Man without Gall* (acholos)

That a dependent, especially a slave, must endure injustice, insults, and beatings without being able to put up a defense is a topic which is discussed in various connections. On the one hand it was suggested that the ethical stance of the master is quite different from that of the slave. A master will not stand for injustice and insult. If he puts up with it he is open to criticism for behaving like a slave.[44] On the other hand it was recommended that the underdog should make a virtue out of necessity, for "often it doesn't pay to avenge injustice."[45] Seneca relates startling instances of this attitude. For example, he tells the story of a Roman nobleman whose son the emperor had condemned to death for no valid reason and then asked the father to dinner: "The poor wretch went through with it, although he seemed to be drinking the blood of his son . . . Do you ask why? He had a second son."[46] Again, the injunction to avoid litigation in one's own or other people's interests as well as the further injunction to requite evil with good and to treat one's enemy justly, as we find it in the Babylonian "Counsels of Wisdom," belong to the same context. They are common sense rules for the little man.[47]

However different the specific context may be, in all of these cases the acceptance of injustice on the part of dependents springs precisely from their position of dependence. In early Christian teaching slaves are advised to put up even with injustice at the hands of their masters without resisting (1 Pet. 2:18ff. and perhaps also Col. 3:25). Athenagoras also reports with great pride that one can find among Christians simple folk such as artisans and old women who show their enemies the love which Christianity requires of them by their good deeds. When struck, they do not strike back. When robbed, they do not take it to court.[48] Athenagoras regards this attitude as a meritorious act. He never notices that such behavior is the inevitable consequence of their dependent state, an imperative arising from necessity. He implicitly assumes that these people have their options open. It does not do justice to the situation to argue that the virtue born of despair is enhanced by religious and ethical considerations or to argue that Christian ethics here becomes the self-appointed advocate of the social order (although it can hardly be denied that this is just what happens in other early Christian texts). In this instance the hero is not the obedient person but the victim of injustice. Why such an attitude should be singled out for praise cannot be discerned from what we have seen so far. Yet it does suggest a negative conclusion. Neither 1 Pet. 2:18ff. nor Athenagoras nor even Matt. 5:38ff. refer to the situation of dependency as the cause of the attitude which it enjoins. In this they are quite unlike those ancient texts we cited above from antiquity as examples of patient endurance on the part of the dependent. Consequently these Christian texts were quite unaware that it was their powerlessness which played a determinative role in the subject's behavior. An attitude of submission subject to the contempt of the aristocrat or to the sympathy and regrets of a Seneca is elevated here with surprising assurance as the ideal, but without taking into account the relation of dependence.

All of this leads us to ask whether it makes any sense to consider social distinctions in interpreting the ethical teaching of early Christianity. We can see from 1 Pet. 2:18ff. and from Athenagoras how in the last resort the ethical attitude of the dependent is left unconnected with the specific situation of dependence. Should we therefore ignore such social differences, and assume that Matt. 5:38ff. par. inculcates a universal ethic intended for everyone under all circumstances? If so, it leads us to another consideration.

b) The Renunciation of Revenge by the Powerful

This is a constant theme in classical ethics. "It is not honourable, as in acts of kindness, to requite benefits with benefits, so to requite injuries with injuries. In the one case it is shameful to be outdone, in the other not to be outdone. 'Revenge' is an inhuman word, and 'retaliation' is not much different from injustice except in degree."[49] If we abstract ethical considerations from the particular social context, then the sentiments of Seneca offer a close parallel to the early Christian teaching on renouncing revenge and loving the enemy.[50] The enemy must receive pardon and assistance.[51] The renunciation of revenge is understood to be not merely refraining from doing harm to one's enemy. It is also a positive act of kindness. In his treatise *On Anger* Seneca outlines an ethic for the wise man who undertakes public office. He is to act as a fair judge.[52] He must not give way to anger but punishes justly and heals. His aim is the welfare of society (II, xxxi.7). It is not exaggerated self-love (II, xxxi.3) that influences his actions, but nobility of heart: "He is a great and noble man who acts as does the lordly wild beast that listens unconcernedly to the baying of tiny dogs."[53] "The ability to bear insults [is] a great help in the maintenance of a throne."[54] This applies to the rulers of the state as well as to the masters of households: "What right have I to make my slave atone by stripes and manacles for too loud a reply . . . Many have pardoned their enemies; shall I not pardon the lazy, the careless, and the babbler?"[55]

The political experiences of Rome, both at home and abroad, with the enemies she had subjugated, showed that refraining from revenge and wrath preserved the body politic, the empire (II, xxxiv.4).[56] Seneca's *On Anger* depicts the role of the conscientious pater-familias, the upper class citizen who behaves like a fair judge in the Roman household, and whose freedom is guaranteed by the law.[57] The role of the emperor, shaped as it is by clemency, would seem to be analogous.[58] In practice the clemency of the emperor is the same as equinimity. It means refraining from revenge and retribution. Clemency "means restraining the mind from vengeance when it has the power to take it or the leniency of a superior toward an inferior in fixing punishment."[59] In other words, it is a "surrogate for the loss of civil liberty."[60] Or again in the domestic sphere it is a substitute for the legal protection which the victim lacks in face of parental authority.

In these writings Seneca addresses himself to ethical problems which were widely discussed in classical times. They involve the ideology of political power and ethical codes for rulers as the traditional theme of refraining from anger.[61] Isocrates and Plutarch as well as Themistios and Julian[62] all teach renunciation of revenge and of retribution on the part of the ruler. The same idea is also found in the ethics of Hellenistic Judaism.[63] Although there is a close similarity between some of these ethical injunctions addressed to the head of the state or of a household and those of Matt. 5:38 par., there can be no doubt that Matt. 5:38ff. presupposes a fundamentally different situation. This is not because the Jesus tradition requires only *love* of the enemy,[64] but because the attitude of kindness shown by the stronger party to the dependent weaker person does not do justice to the social conditions of early Christianity; nor (if one tries to imagine the power relationships obtaining between Christians and their presecutors) is there anything to suggest it in the text of Matt. 5:38ff. par. Nothing is said of any fault on the part of the dependents. True, the allusion to the imitation of God in Matt. 5:45 par. and the requirement of generosity in Matt. 5:42 are popular and typical features in the ideology of power.[65] But no one would doubt that Matt. 5:38ff. par. does not deal with grace toward the conquered enemy because such grace of the stronger party has as its purpose the preservation of its dominance over others. When we speak of the universality of the commandment to love the enemy and thereby assume that "everybody knows" what has to be done,[66] this is not the cynicism of power (even the power of the humane ruler). But it does mean that when we describe things that way we are presupposing social differences even if they are not explicitly mentioned or regarded as unimportant. When we ignore the social relationship that exists between the subjects who love and the objects of their love, then Matt. 5:38ff. par. is open to misunderstanding, and is ambiguous in a way that invites misuse.

c) Nonviolence: The Protest of the Powerless

Neither love of the enemy as the exercise of one's own power, nor love of the enemy as the resignation to one's own powerlessness captures the sense of Matt. 5:38ff. Since we can start with the powerlessness of the people addressed in Matt. 5:38, it is of interest for the interpretation of this text to notice that there exists a strain of ethical teaching in antiquity which also describes the non-violence of the powerless but understands it as an act of protest.

Plato interprets Socrates' acceptance of his death sentence as a renunciation of vengeance, a refusal to requite injustice in kind.[67] Socrates refuses to flee from execution because that would be substituting one wrong for another. It would be wrong because it would be an act of rebellion against the law—"it is impious to use violence against either your father or your mother, and much more impious to use it against your country."[68] The alternatives are either to obey or to convince your country where true justice lies. The laws are still valid even when they are executed by evil men. Socrates, who is acting solely for the well-being of the state, faces his accusers defenseless. "I shall be like a doctor tried by a bunch of children on a charge brought by a cook."[69] Socrates is "the only righteous man who is not able to defend himself against the corruption of a state that has become completely unjust."[70]

Socrates figures in many legends of antiquity as the symbol of the philosopher who is brutally treated by society and who can only respond by protesting in powerlessness.[71] The surrounding world in the eyes of the philosopher is a world of wild beasts: "But Socrates, when Aristocrates had kicked him, accused him of nothing else but of saying to those who passed by 'This man is sick with the sickness of mules.' "[72] This and similar legends about renunciation of violence on the part of the philosopher are widespread in antiquity.[73] It is undoubtedly difficult to assign them to a specific social context since they are also used as models for renunciation of revenge by rulers. But Plutarch correctly senses that they do not fit too well into this context. The absence of anger, he observes, is the victory of the strong: "For this reason I always strive to collect and to peruse, not only those sayings and deeds of the philosophers, who are said by fools to have no bile but even more those of kings and despots."[74]

We shall not do justice to all these legends, which are told especially of Socrates, Antisthenes, Diogenes of Sinope, and Crates, if we interpret them in the framework of the texts in which they occur. But we can recapture a stereotyped pattern: the philosopher is beaten or abused because he is a disconcerting teacher. Majestically he refuses to hit back and publishes a *bon mot* or a pamphlet, declaring that he has been the victim of injustice. It is especially the protests of the Cynics that are correctly reproduced in these legends. "Even in its noblest representatives, this attitude was never anything else but a practical protest of individuals against the sufferings, follies and sins of a civilization which had grown rigid, which had lost its soul, and was ripe for destruction. It was an attempt to save the liberty of the individual from the general shipwreck."[75] Epictetus also uses these motifs in his portrayal of the Cynics, though not in the form of legends.[76] They all revolve around the principle that the individual is confronted by a crowd of madmen, beasts, or misguided children. He accepts their blows without resisting in order to proclaim the rottenness of society, not only in words but also in his body. If we compare these legends with Matt. 5:38ff. par. the difference is clear. It is important for the understanding of the ethical teaching of the synoptics that the subject addressed is not an isolated individual, but a member of the Christian community.

THE LOVE OF CHRISTIANS FOR THEIR PERSECUTORS

The call to non-violence, renunciation of revenge and love of the enemy has come down to us in several different versions. In their Lucan and Matthean forms they allow us to reconstruct the common tradition which lies behind them. Such a reconstruction is inevitably conjectural to some extent. For instance, we do not know the original order of the injunctions, yet all the stages of the tradition are in substantial agreement.

a) The Command to Love the Enemy

The tradition common to Matthew and Luke already defined "your enemies" as "those who persecute you."[77] The Christian should love the persecutors of Christians. Rom. 12:14 shows that the words "bless those who curse you" in Luke 6:28 are substantially pre-Lucan. Whether this phrase already existed in Q remains uncertain. However, it is substantially identical with the prayer for the persecutors which already occurs in Q. Even there persecution must include calumny and social ostracism as the verb "to curse"[78] shows. Moreover, the parallel material in Luke 6:22 par.; Rom. 12:14; 1 Cor. 4:12f.; 1 Pet. 2:12, 23; 3:9, 16; 4:4, 14 makes the same point. Neither Luke nor Matthew made any significant alterations in the way the enemies are regarded.[79] Again, the attitude of love a Christian is expected to show toward the enemies of the community is very much the same in all layers of the tradition. When Luke speaks of doing good in 6:27 and 35 we may assume that he is trying to express the commandment to love the enemy in terms more intelligible to the Hellenistic world and its ethical vocabulary,[80] yet without changing the essential notion. The "concrete, active character of this love, which emerges in social intercourse,"[81] is equally applicable to "doing good to," "praying for," "blessing" one's enemies.[82] The Christian is challenged to include his persecutor in his own community, the community of life together which is awaiting the coming salvation. But of course the Christians' enemies are human beings who reject and refuse this invitation and on their part wish to detach themselves. Consequently the command to love the enemy is thoroughly aggressive though not in a destructive sense. The enemies are to abandon their enmity; in other words, they must undergo a change of attitude. The command to love the enemy is an appeal to take up a missionary attitude toward one's persecutors. This brings out the universal all-embracing claim of the salvation offered by Christianity. Even the enemies of the community are to be given a place in its common life and in the kingly rule of God. This challenge may not have pleased their enemies at all. Hence it is only partly true to say that love of the enemy is the central content of the Christian proclamation. It is certainly also a *means* for mission and conversion. If we were to define what the Christian message is all about, there is one point we should have to include. This is that the expected salvation is for all. This makes a difference to the practice of the Christian life. "Overcome evil with good" (Rom. 12:21)— that is exactly what it means to love the enemy. The aim is to conquer him, not "to surrender oneself into the hands of evil."[83] Since there is no claim to domination here the ambiguity of the idea of loving the enemy can only be cleared up by taking social distinctions into account. The desire of the powerless for the salvation of their enemies is the precise opposite of the desire of the ruling classes to integrate their enemies or rebellious subjects into their dominion after they have defeated them.

Later Christian modifications of the commandment to love the enemy confirm the interpretation proposed here, despite some shifts of emphasis. The enemy must be won over.[84] He must be persuaded to lead a different kind of life,[85] and to participate in the Christian hope.

Does this teaching go back to the historical Jesus? Given the character of our sources it would be more than hypothetical to suppose it does.[86] But even if we leave the historical question aside, such a reconstruction does not seem to involve any serious change in the interpretation of the commandment to love the enemy when compared with the more clearly recognizable stages of the tradition so long as we assume that the identification of "your enemies" with "your persecutors" goes back to the historical Jesus.[87] If, however, this identification is to be regarded as secondary,[88] then we would have, as an authentic saying of Jesus, the command "Love your enemies," and the promise of becoming sons of God attached to it. This command continues to be open to all sorts of interpretations so long as it remains unclear who precisely the enemies are. What Lührmann has done is to give specific content to this multifaceted saying by invoking the tradition about Jesus' attitude toward sinners.[89] Matt. 5:45 calls into question the hostility of the enemy and with it one's own righteousness. "Refusal to insist on one's own rights is demanded as the will of God."[90] But I do not think that Matt. 5:44a—45 can be filled out in this way. This is because although the saying is very short it can be taken in many different ways. It does not encourage doubt about the hostility of the enemy or the unrighteousness of the unrighteous on whom God sends sun and rain. What the commandment requires is that we should love our enemies even though they truly are our enemies.

b) Avoiding Contact with "Sinners"

This concern is present in all recognizable stages of the tradition. Even in Q, as the agreements between Matt. 5:46–47 and Luke 6:32–35 show, the rhetorical questions indicate that a distinction should be drawn between Christians and non-Christians.[91] Christians should love others even when they refuse to reciprocate. The love of the enemy is a distinctively Christian attitude, something poles apart from the non-Christian attitude of "requiting love with love" and "doing good in return." The variations on this theme in Matthew and Luke make no difference to its meaning, not even Luke's somewhat clumsy illustrations as, for instance, when he speaks about "lending." His purpose here is to make it clear that there is no question of reciprocity.[92] This distinction affirms that everyone who is not subject to Jesus' teaching practices only recip- rocal love. In drawing this distinction Luke reminds us of that pop- ular figure in antiquity, the loyal citizen: "A man's virtue is this— that he be competent to manage the affairs of his city, and manage them so as to benefit his friends and harm his enemies."[93] In shaping the antitheses Matthew has once more taken up this idea in his contrast between the love for the neighbor and hatred of the enemy (Matt. 5:43). Matthew's antithesis to the Old Testament and to Judaism ignores the fact that hatred of the enemy[94] is a common expression of clan solidarity in antiquity.

The train of thought in Matt. 5:46–47 and Luke 6:32–35 is as follows: Christian identity is unique compared with that of all other human groups, so far as the obligation to love the enemy is con- cerned. Christians should reach out beyond the limits of group solidarity and in so doing find their own identity as a group. Here is a paradox, which becomes a flat contradiction[95] only when the search for identity results in an exclusiveness which leads to an un- loving attitude toward the non-Christian. But that is not the mean- ing here. Insistence on the love of enemy has a public and implic- itly political dimension because it explicitly refers to the identity of the social group.

c) Non-Violence

In Matt. 5:39–42 par. we have several illustrations of the accept- ance of injustice without resorting to self-defense.[96] Thus the point at issue is the way we treat our enemy. Since the injustice involved is illustrated by a number of examples, only the context can show what particular kind of enemy the text has in view (i.e., from Matt. 5:44–45 par.). Even if we can no longer reconstruct the original order in Q of these sayings about non-violence and the love of the enemy[97] this much is clear. In all strata of the tradition both concepts stand side by side and were regarded as variations on a common theme. In Luke the examples of non-violence are arranged in such a way that they become illustrations of the love of enemy. But also in Matthew where the material has been shaped into two independent antitheses the similarity of their meaning is undeniable. Both concepts are concerned with the treatment of the enemy. To be sure, the two attitudes demanded cannot easily be combined. If one takes non-resistance in the face of injustice as the starting point for defining the meaning of love for the enemy, then the renunciation of all claims on the part of the loving subject becomes the focal point. And when that happens you cannot really make sense of Matt. 5:44–45 par., which enjoins the love of the enemy.[98] If one starts with Matt. 5:44–45 par. and takes the love of enemy as an active love, then the injunction to accept injustice becomes an enigma. Non-resistance, total surrender to the enemy's unjust demands, can hardly be called love. If it is taken as a universally applicable ethic, the enigma is insoluble. Yet the two injunctions—love for the enemy and non-violence—must be brought together since the context demands it.

A solution will only be possible if we bear in mind the concrete situations in early Christianity to which these injunctions apply. This means we must take the line of Martin Hengel and P. Hoffmann.[99]

Non-resistance must be applied concretely in the area of politics. In this way Matt. 5:39–41 par. would have been understood in two different ways, the one within the community and the other toward outsiders. Within the community it would mean refusing to plan an insurrection or to put up a show of violent resistance. Toward those outside it would mean assuring everyone of peaceable intentions, making a political apology: We Christians are not revolutionaries. Thus Matt. 5:39–41 par. would function similarly to Rom. 13:1–7 and Mark 12:17 par. The injunction "Do not resist one who is evil," with which Matthew summarizes his illustration of non-violence, would then mean refusing to put up a certain type of resistance.[100] Or, in other words, the "non-cooperation with evil" of which Martin Luther King spoke is not incompatible with Matt. 5:39.[101] This is because Matt. 5:39 is not a fundamental rejection of *every* type of resistance.

This hypothesis is supported in the Christian tradition in early post-New Testament times. The commandment to love the enemy often appears in connection with the type of political apology mentioned above.[102] In a similar vein, 1 Pet. 2:13ff. establishes a political context for the passive resistance of injustice. It hardly seems accidental that the injunctions in Rom. 12:14, 17, and 19–21 inculcate in effect the love of the enemy, and that Rom. 13:1–7 regulates the Christian attitude to the state.[103] The political apology in these passages is not to be confused with a subordinationist morality. As I see it, Tertullian hit the nail on the head when he explained the command to love the enemy in his *Apology*. On the one hand he assures his readers that Christians never take revenge when they become the victims of injustice. Such a thing never takes the form of nocturnal attacks or open revolt or even of passive resistance. Yet on the other hand Christians are factors of resistance in society. To be sure, they are not enemies of the human race, but opponents of human error.[104]

REFLECTIONS ON
THE THEOLOGICAL SIGNIFICANCE

When we consider the theological significance of the love of enemy and the practice of non-violence, we must always take social distinctions into account. As we have seen, it is impossible to understand the teaching of Jesus about the love of enemy as we find it in the gospels if we ignore those distinctions. We must take into account how the loving subject and his enemy relate to one another socially, in the field of tension created by the power which the one party exercises over the other. Such social analysis is indispensable if we are to understand the teaching of Jesus as it was preserved in early Christianity. The same is true if we are concerned with our own identity as Christians today. Any basic discussion of the problem of power which seeks to describe a given attitude as Christian, for everyone and under all circumstances, inevitably remains ambiguous, even if it tries to avoid ambiguity. Neither making absolute demands upon others nor requiring non-resistance on the part of Christians who occupy positions of power, imposed upon those who are powerless, can be taken as the authentic application of the early Christian teaching of the love of enemy. The limitations of passive resistance (especially in dictatorships) are all too familiar. There can be no doubt that for disciples of Christ non-resistance is an essential part of their life-style. But our assent to non-resistance is only credible when pursued in combination with the practice of resistance, and where it is a combative and evangelistic means for the salvation of all. The cry for a necessary share of power on the one hand and on the other the cry for absolute non-violence (we have heard a lot about that in the discussion about racism) have often been misapplied because the prevailing social differences were conveniently ignored.[105]

NOTES

1. So H. Schürmann, *Das Lukasevangelium* I (Freiburg, 1969), 342; A. Nissen, *Gott und der Nächste im antiken Judentum: Untersuchungen zum Doppelgebot der Liebe* (Tübingen, 1974), 303–4. D. Lührmann, "Liebet eure Feinde," *ZTK* 69 (1972), 426. The notion is so common that we need give no further references. Interpretations of the love of enemy as a cosmopolitan philanthropy often end up in a paraphrase which changes its whole meaning. E.g., it is said that a person must "also" or "even" love his enemy. See W. Trilling, *Das Evangelium nach Matthäus* (Düsseldorf, 1962), 135.

2. R. Bultmann, *Jesus and the Word* (New York, 1958), 112.

3. R. Bultmann, 112.

4. R. Bultmann, 112.

5. R. Bultmann, 113.

6. R. Bultmann, 92.

7. R. Bultmann, 114.

8. These instructions for behavior inculcating renunciation of revenge and intercessory prayer have been relativized by Bultmann, 117. He prefers to take forgiveness as the renunciation of any personal claim.

9. Actually, Bultmann does lay more stress on the connection between the injunction to love the enemy as we find it in early Christianity and similar injunctions in the ethics of non-Christian antiquity. In this he is better than much recent exegesis. One recent exception is G. Strecker, *Handlungsorientierter Glaube* (Stuttgart, 1972), 46, 67. Bultmann perceives that the commandment of love for the enemy is by no means "new" in the history of human thought. See his *Jesus,* 111 and his "Das christliche Gebot der Nächstenliebe," in *Glauben und Verstehen* I (Tübingen, 1954), 236–37, 243. But for Bultmann the contrast he draws between the love of enemy in the Sermon on the Mount and e.g., in Seneca, does not serve any didactic function. Its function is rather theological. In the Bible it is not an ethical demand, for that would mean an ethic of achievement. See e.g., *Jesus,* 93.

10. H. Braun, *Spätjüdisch-häretischer und frühchristlicher Radikalismus* II (Tübingen, 1957), 91.

11. H. Braun, 91 and *idem, Jesus* (Stuttgart, 1969), 130.

12. H. Braun, *Jesus,* 130; *Radikalismus,* 91, note 2.

13. H. Braun, *Jesus,* 131; *Radikalismus,* 91f.

14. H. Braun, *Radikalismus,* 57, note 1; 91, note 2; *Jesus,* 125, 130.

15. H. Braun, *Jesus,* 130.

16. H. Braun, *Jesus,* 124. H. Conzelmann, *An Outline of the Theology of the New Testament* (London, 1969), 121 takes this to imply "the absoluteness of the commandment." He goes on to say, "I can no longer ask whether 'I must' offer the other cheek. In that case, the further question, when I need not do so, would be in the background."

17. H. Braun, *Jesus,* 124.

18. H. Braun, *Jesus,* 125.

19. J. Weiss and W. Bousset, *Die drei älteren Evangelien* (Göttingen, 1917), 271. Cf. J. Weiss, *Die Predigt Jesu vom Reiche Gottes* (Göttingen, ³1964), 148–50 [omitted from ET, which is from the 1892 ed.]

20. H. Schürmann, 344, 349. Schürmann defines the enemy as far as the older stages of the tradition are concerned and for Matthew, too, as religious enemies. He does not see any tension between this interpretation and that which speaks of love always and for everyone. See also 202–33, note 29.

21. See also Martin Luther King, *Strength to Love* (New York/Evanston/London, 1963), 34–41.

22. On this see esp. T. Ebert, *Gewaltfreier Aufstand. Alternative zum Bürgerkrieg* (Düsseldorf, 1969).

23. M. L. King, 40.

24. See the above quotation from J. Weiss, *Predigt,* 200–01; Schürmann, *Lukasevangelium,* 349.

25. On this see T. Ebert, 33; H. J. Benedict, "Licht und Finsternis" in T. Ebert and H. J. Benedict (eds.), *Macht von unten* (Hamburg, 1968), 60–73. This essay deals with the assassination of Martin Luther King and its consequences as reflected in the German press.

26. M. L. King, *Strength to Love,* 40.

27. J. Weiss, *Evangelien,* 268–69. It is not always right to fight.

For such cases the prohibition of resistance is a mode of "training" for "self-mastery" and "renunciation."

28. See above, note 20.

29. H. Schürmann, 342, 347–48: "He who always acts thus in such cases evidently no longer has any interest in his own ego. He has given up self-love entirely" (348). This hope, he says, is the "interior presupposition" for creative love of the enemy (347).

30. P. Hoffmann, *Studien der Theologie der Logienquelle* (Münster, 1976), 76. See also Lührmann, 437; G. Baumbach, *Das Verständnis des Bösen in den synoptischen Evangelien* (Berlin, 1963), 70

31. M. Hengel, *Was Jesus a Revolutionist?* (Facet Books; Philadelphia, 1971), 28.

32. M. Hengel, 28–29. I cannot, however, agree with Hengel's (and Martin Luther King's) treatment of Jesus as a non-violent peacemaker between two warring factions on the "left and right" (see esp. 28). Nor can I see the point of the alternatives he offers in a discussion with Helmut Gollwitzer, viz., *either* Camillo Torres *or* Martin Luther King (see 32, note 87). After all, non-violence involves insurrection and resistance. Martin Luther King drew a distinction between violence directed against property and violence directed against persons. He never understood his movement as a pacifist one in any doctrinaire sense. He spoke of a "realistic pacifism . . . which in the prevailing circumstances must be regarded as the lesser evil . . . I do not claim to be free from the contradiction to which every Christian non-pacifist is exposed." Hengel does not realize that he is just as inconsistent himself when he says that emergency measures for self-protection are justified (32, note 87) and that Gollwitzer sees an important point in this inconsistency. It cannot be disposed of by dogmatically recommending non-resistance to those whose injustices we do not share. Nor can we keep silent when we are involved in violence, even if we do not actually bear arms. On these questions see esp. H. Gollwitzer, "Zum Problem der Gewalt in der christlichen Ethik" in H. G. Geyer (ed.) *Freispruch und Freiheit: Theologische Aufsätze für W. Kreck* (Munich, 1973), 148–67.

33. E.g., A. Wlosok, *Rom und die Christen* (Stuttgart, 1970).

34. "Counsels of Wisdom," lines 31–48 in W. G. Lambert, *Babylonian Wisdom Literature* (Oxford, 1960), 101; "Lehre des Amenemope" IV 10–V 6 (ANET), 422; for the OT see e.g., 1 Sam. 24:18; Exod. 23:4–5; Prov. 24:17, 29; 25:21–22. For post-biblical Judaism see A. Nissen, *Gott,* 304–29; for Greek and Roman literature see M. Waldmann, *Die Feindesliebe in der antiken Welt und im Christentum* (Vienna, 1902), 19–88; A. Dihle, *Die goldene Regel* (Göttingen, 1962), 41–79 (on the abandonment of the idea of revenge); W. C. van Unnik, "Die Feindesliebe in Lukas VI 32–35," *NovTest* 8 (1966), 284–300. On gentleness toward one's enemies in the Old Testament see also Philo, *De virtutibus,* 109–20. Celsus and Origen were already concerned about the relation between the Sermon on the Mount and Plato. See Origen, *Contra Celsum* VII, 58.

35. See e.g., the literature cited in note 34.

36. Justin, *Apology* I, 15 changes the rhetorical question in Matt. 5:46–47 into "What do you do that is new?"

37. Rom. 12:19–20; Justin, *Dialogue* 85, 7; Theophilus, *Ad Autolycum* III, 14.

38. Athenagoras, *Legatio* 12; Justin, *Apology* I, 15, 1 "to show affection to all"; Cf. *Epistle of Diognetus* V, 11.

39. I know of no instance where agape is directed to the enemy in the non-Christian world. Seneca would seem occasionally to come quite close to it. See R. Bultmann above, note 9; Waldmann, 67–75; Dihle, 71; cf. further Epictetus, *Discourses* III, xxii, 54: "For this too is a very pleasant strand woven into the Cynic's pattern of life; he must needs be flogged like an ass, and while he is being flogged he must love the men who flog him, as though he were the father or brother of them all" (Loeb tr.).

40. See e.g., A. Dihle, 72.

41. A. Nissen, 315–16.

42. When Nissen draws up his series of contrasts (e.g., on 314, "Overcoming of self in favor of the other is not however self-surrender contrary to self-interest, readiness to forgive . . . is not abandonment of one's rightful claims . . .") it creates at the very least the impression that the difference involves a further

value judgment. The question as to why early Christianity in this instance opted for an alternative view would then have to be raised. Only so could we avoid the suspicion of implying the superiority of Christianity. There is a long tradition behind this question and the way it was handled in the comparative study of religions by Christian interpreters and especially those who, like Nissen, want to do justice to the other religion.

43. Seneca, *De Ira* II, xxxiv, 1.

44. Callicles in Plato, *Gorgias* 483B; Aristotle, *Nicomachean Ethics* IV, 11; Theophrastus, *Characters* 1; see also the quotations from Theophrastus in Seneca, *De Ira* (e.g., I, xiv, 1). Further material in Nissen, *Gott,* 306; Dihle, 33.

45. Seneca, *De Ira* II, xxxiii, 2 (Loeb tr.).

46. Seneca, *De Ira* II, xxxiii, 3–4 (Loeb tr.). See also *De Ira* III, xiv f.

47. For the sources see note 34. On the interpretation see W. G. Lambert, "Morals in Ancient Mesopotamia," *JEOL* 5 (1955–58), 188.

48. Athenagoras, *Legatio,* 11. Cf., ET by W. R. Schoedel (Oxford, 1972) *ad loc.*

49. Seneca, *De Ira* II, xxxii, 1.

50. As such, they are noted by e.g., Bultmann, Waldmann, and Dihle.

51. On this point see also Seneca, *De Otio* i ,4 and *De Ira* III, xxiv, 2.

52. For further discussions of this theme see e.g., *De Ira* II, xxvi, 6; xxviii, 1; III, xxvi, 3.

53. II, xxxii, 3 (Loeb tr.).

54. III, xxiii, 2 (Loeb tr.).

55. III, xxiv, 3 (Loeb tr.).

56. On this political background of the clemency of the prince and its variants see J. Kabiersch, *Untersuchungen zum Begriff der Philanthropia bei dem Kaiser Julian* (Wiesbaden, 1960), 15ff.; T. Adam, *Clementia Principis* (Stuttgart, 1970), 82ff.; M. Fuhrmann, "Die Alleinherrschaft und das Problem der Gerechtigkeit," *Gymnasium* 70 (1963), esp. 508.

57. On this see esp. Fuhrmann.

58. Cf. e.g., *De Clementia* I, v, 1 with *De Ira* II, xxxi, 7–8, both of which use the metaphor of the body and its members when speaking of renouncing revenge against human beings who have done wrong.

59. Seneca, *De Clementia* II, iii, 1.

60. Fuhrmann, 510.

61. On the tradition behind the theme *De Ira* see A. Bourgery, "Introduction," in *Sénèque, Dialogues* part 1, *De Ira* (Paris, 1951), v–xxiv.

62. Isocrates *To Nicocles* 23; Plutarch, *De Cohibenda Ira, passim;* F. Taeger, *Charisma* 2 (Stuttgart, 1960), 78; K. Winkler, art. "Clementia" in *Reallexikon für Antike und Christentum* 3, 206–31.

63. *Letter of Aristeas* 227. In *Joseph and Aseneth,* too, we find that the renunciation of revenge on the part of the God-fearing person is regarded as an act of grace toward his defeated enemies (23,9; 28,7; 29, 3–5) following the divisions of P. Riessler, *Altjüdisches Schrifttum ausserhalb der Bibel* (Augsburg, 1927). On 23,12 see Nissen, 310, note 967.

64. This contrast is often emphasized. See e.g., Waldmann, 66. But this pays too much attention to the actual wording. This is because the renunciation of revenge on the part of the stronger party means showing mercy and assistance, and performing remedial action. On this see note 39 above.

65. There are close parallels to Matt. 5:45 in Seneca, *De Beneficiis* IV, xxvi 1; Marcus Aurelius IX, ix, 27. On this popular theme see H. D. Betz, *Nachfolge und Nachahmung Jesu Christi im Neuen Testament* (Tübingen, 1967), 121–36; H. A. Fischel, *Rabbinic Literature and Greco-Roman Philosophy* (Leiden, 1973), 92–93; Kabiersch, 30, 39, 53–61; Nissen, 69–76; R. Mach, *Der Zaddik in Talmud und Midrasch* (Leiden, 1957) 20–22; On the theme of generosity see Kabiersch, 34ff.

66. Bultmann, *Jesus,* 112; also H. Conzelmann, 121: "Offering the other cheek is not an attitude; it can be meaningful only in the act."

67. Plato, *Crito* 49A ff.; for the interpretation see R. Guardini, *Der Tod des Sokrates* (Hamburg, 1956), 85ff.; P. Friedländer, *Platon* II, 162ff.

68. Plato, *Crito* 51C (Loeb tr.).

69. Plato, *Gorgias* 521 E (Loeb tr.).

70. O. Gigon, *Sokrates* (Berne, 1947).

71. O. Gigon supposes that the motif of Socrates' defenselessness antedates Plato.

72. Themistios, *On Virtue* (Greek text ed. J. Gildemeister and F. Bücheler, *Rhenisches Museum* 27 [1872]), 461.

73. Collections of such legends used as examples will be found e.g., in Themistios, 459–62; Seneca, *De Ira* III, xi, 2; xxxviii, 1; Plutarch, *De Cohibenda Ira* 14; Diogenes Laertius VI, 33, 89, 90; II, 21.

74. Plutarch, *De Cohibenda Ira* 9 (Loeb tr.).

75. J. Bernays, *Lucian und die Kyniker* (Berlin, 1879), 25.

76. See above, note 39.

77. Although the exact wording is uncertain, the difference between "persecute," (Matt. 5:44) and "abuse" (Luke 6:28) is negligible.

78. On the use of the curse to ostracize from society see Plutarch *Alcibiades* 22; Also W. Schottroff, *Der altisraelitische Fluchspruch* (Neukirchen, 1969), 206–10. For the love of enemy as social acceptance where such acceptance is refused or ruled out because of social barriers John 4:7–9 would be sufficient example. Similarly, Justin, *Apology* I, xiv, 3 places praying for one's enemies alongside of social acceptance beyond the limits of prevailing convention. Regarding *Acts of the Scillitan Martyrs* we may also ask whether the martyrs' claim, "Numquam maledixious," which served to justify political loyalty to the emperor, does not imply the same idea. Despite the bad treatment meted out to them, the Christians still regarded themselves as full members of pagan society.

79. It is sometimes said that Luke, unlike Q and Matthew, is thinking of personal enemies. According to Schürmann, 345, Luke 6:29–30 shifts the reference to the private sphere (though these verses are only illustrations and cannot be used to define the enemies in question). He claims that the Lucan redaction in 6:34–35a supports this interpretation (but the words "lending" and "doing good" are hardly enough to tip the scales). According to J. Weiss, 270–71 (cf. also W. Bauer, "Das Gebot der Fein-

desliebe und die alten Christen," *ZTK* 27 [1917]). esp. 38, repr. in *Aufsätze und kleine Schriften ZTK* 27 (Tübingen, 1967), esp. 236, the terms Luke uses for enmity are more general in character. Yet even the verb "to hate," which is peculiarly Lucan, still lies within the parameters of persecution terminology. On the latter see H. Braun, *Radikalismus* I, 107, note 4; H. Schürmann, 345, note 15. It cannot be ascribed to Luke with any certainty. See O. H. Steck, *Israel und das gewaltsame Geschick der Propheten* (Neukirchen, 1967), 22–23, note 4.

For Q we may assume that the main concern is for conflicts with the Jews. See S. Schulz, *Q, Die Spruchquelle der Evangelisten* (Zürich, 1972), 455. For Matthew and Luke it is more likely that the conflicts are those between the Christians and their pagan neighbors. On Matthew see esp. G. Strecker, *Der Weg der Gerechtigkeit* (Göttingen, 1971), 30; for Luke see H. Conzelmann, *The Theology of St. Luke* (New York, 1960), 233–34.

80. This was argued persuasively by van Unnik, esp. 295, 297–98.

81. Van Unnik, 298.

82. It would be wrong to limit these injunctions to the emotions. For a Jew or Christian love has something to do with the Torah and recalls Lev. 19:18. Applications like those in Matt. 5:42 par. and Luke 6:34–35 (giving and lending) are only meant as illustrations, though they do make clear the active character of love.

83. This is how A. Nissen, 314 characterizes Christian love for the enemy in contrast to Jewish statements on the subject. There is a further question as to whether there are not certain Jewish texts (esp. Test XII Patr. and Slavonic Enoch) which express an attitude to the enemy similar to what we have found in the early Christian tradition about Jesus.

84. 1 Pet. 2:12 is also the theme of 2:18ff. And although "to gain" (3:1) concerns the attitude of Christian women to their non-Christian husbands, its affinity with 2:18ff. is unmistakable.

85. Justin, *Apology* I, 14,3; 57:1; cf. Aristides, *Apology* 15:5; 17:3.

86. Cf. L. Schottroff, "Der Mensch Jesus im Spannungsfeld von politischer Theologie und Aufklärung," *ThP* 8 (1973), esp. 244.

87. See also e.g., R. Bultmann, *History of the Synoptic Tradition* (Oxford, 1972), 79; H. Braun, *Radikalismus,* II, 91 note 2.

88. So Lührmann, 426. His arguments are possible so far as the history of the tradition is concerned, but not compelling: 1. The questions in Matt. 5:46–47. par. make no reference to Matt. 5:44b and are a secondary addition to an older and simpler version of the injunction; 2. Matt. 5:44a is to Matt. 5:44b as Luke 6:20b, 21 is to Luke 6:22–23. Hence the situation of persecution seems to be a secondary addition here as well.

89. Lührmann, 437.

90. Lührmann, 432.

91. The "taxcollectors" and "Gentiles" or "sinners" are equivalent to "non-Christians," as the context makes clear. They include all who do not practice love for their enemies. Which of the substantives goes back to Q is an open question. In Luke 6:32–34 the question, "what credit is that to you?" must be interpreted as a hope for divine approbation in view of the considerations mentioned in note 93. See the pertinent arguments in van Unnik, 295–97; H. Conzelmann, *TDNT* IX, 392.

92. To lend "expecting nothing in return" of course means in practice to give. There is no question of the payment of interest. The awkward phrase "to receive as much again" led to emendations quite early in the MS tradition. Luke means reciprocity of relationship, whether he is thinking of the return of something borrowed or the expectation that the other party will be prepared to lend something in return.

93. Plato, *Meno* 71E (Loeb tr.). There are many instances of this. For example, Plato, *Republic* 336A; Xenophon, *Memorabilia* II, 1, 19 and 21; 2 Sam. 19:7; *Joseph and Aseneth* 24, 7. Further material may be found in H. Bolkestein, *Wohltätigkeit und Armutpflege im vorchristlichen Altertum* (1939; repr. Groningen, 1967); van Unnik, 291–300; Dihle, 32–33; W. Schottroff, 210; Kabiersch, 30–31.

94. We may agree as far as Matt. 5:43 is concerned that the word "to hate" is derived from Lev. 19:18. It would be wrong from both a historical and a theological point of view to treat the problem of clan solidarity as it comes up in Matt. 5:43 as a

specifically OT-Jewish concern. The hatred for outsiders at Qumran (1 QS 1:10; cf. 9:21) with its dualistic accentuation is only one example of group solidarity among others (including those outside of Judaism). The exaggeration here is deliberate. It does not refer to any particular kind of enemy although it is often assumed that it does. Cf., H. Braun, *Qumran und das Neue Testament* I (Tübingen, 1966) 17–18.

95. Thus Lührmann, 426. From a traditio-historical perspective the question arises as to whether Matt. 5:46–47 par. is "secondary," as Bultmann, *History,* 88 alleges, to the command to love the enemy. But in fact it is impossible to deduce any arguments from the context in support of this interpretation.

96. Matt. 5:42 enjoins generosity in giving and lending when the saying is taken in isolation. When, however, it is linked to the preceding verses it is clearly referring to a situation where there is injustice. In other words, it speaks of generosity not only to the needy but also to the impudent. In Luke this verse has been changed to make it quite clear that the reference is to a situation of injustice.

97. Since the order in both Matthew and Luke is the result of deliberate rearrangement all we can say for certain about Q is that it contained both blocks of material. Because it is expressed in the singular, Matt. 5:39–41 differs from Matt. 5:44–45 par., which is in the plural. This means that it may originally have stood as an independent unit. So e.g., Schürmann, 348; Lührmann, 417. But that tells us nothing about what it actually said. For we cannot be certain what enemies it was referring to. Without the context, which is already present in Q, where it is connected with persecutors, Matt. 5:39–41 par. is open to many different applications.

98. See above, pp. 1ff., for the definitions proposed by R. Bultmann and H. Braun.

99. See above, p. 14.

100. For this meaning of "resist" see 1 Macc. 11:38; 14:29, 32. E. Schweizer, *The Good News According to Matthew* (Atlanta, 1975), 129, considered a different application: resistance in a court of law (mainly because of Matt. 5:40). The prohibition against going to court, or the restriction of resort to juridical de-

fense, does have some ethical tradition behind it. See Musonius 10; further material in A. Bonhöffer, *Die Ethik Epiktets* (Stuttgart, 1894); also Athenagoras (see note 48). But in the context of love toward one's persecutors refusal to go to law in self-defense is hardly a plausible injunction.

101. See above, p. 12.

102. See the material in W. Bauer, 42–47; 241–48.

103. Loosely connected moral injunctions linking together traditional ethical themes were formulated not for the concrete needs of a particular community but for the "general requirements of earliest Christendom," M. Dibelius, *From Tradition to Gospel* (London, 1934), 238. The context, however, still leaves open the possibility of a concrete application. "The whole passage is constructed on a logical plan," E. Käsemann, *An die Römer* (HNT 8a; Tübingen, 1973), 310.

104. Tertullian, *Apology* 37.

105. On these problems see above, note 32, and esp. the essay by H. Gollwitzer there mentioned.

REGINALD H. FULLER

The Double Commandment of Love: A Test Case for the Criteria of Authenticity

As is generally known, the double command of love occurs three times in the NT, i.e., once in each of the synoptic Gospels (Mark 12:28–34; Matt. 22:34–40; Luke 10:25–28). Matthew follows Mark in locating the pericope in the Jerusalem ministry, between the Sadducees' question and the Son of David pericope, while Luke places it in the travel section as introduction to the parable of the Good Samaritan.

There are a number of agreements of Matthew and Luke against Mark. Both have "lawyer" instead of Mark's "scribe," and both have "tempting." Both use "in" = "with" with the dative in the list of the faculties with which man is to love God, three times out of three in Matthew and three times out of four in Luke. These parallels often lead to the conclusion, especially among English-speaking scholars,[1] that the double commandment occurs in Q as well as in Mark. The general opinion in these circles is that while Matthew, according to his usual practice, conflates his sources, Luke represents the Q form more or less in its original form, for such a conflation of sources is not normally characteristic of Luke. F. W. Beare carries the argument further and maintains that both Q and the original tradition—exactly as in Luke—attributed the double commandment to the lawyer rather than to Jesus himself.[2] For it is easier to explain the transference of such a saying from Jesus to the lawyer than *vice versa*.

However, on closer examination it is clear that the literary relationship between the three versions of the double commandment is much more complex than it appears to be at first sight.

First, there are more parallels between Matthew and Luke against Mark than Beare has noted. Both evangelists agree in the use of the vocative "teacher" in the introductory question of the lawyer, and in putting the question into direct speech. Both have the expression "in the law" (Luke 10:26; Matt. 22:36) in the introduction and both omit the Shemah (contra Mark 12:29c). Both have the double commandment only once, Matthew as a saying of Jesus, Luke as a pronouncement of the lawyer, whereas in Mark it is expressed for the first time by Jesus and then repeated by the scribe. And finally the two greater evangelists omit the expansion about the superiority of love over burnt offerings which follows the repetition of the double commandment (Mark 12:33 [end]). Thus we have here no less than nine agreements of Luke and Matthew against Mark. This strengthens the view that both Matthew and Luke have used a common tradition,[3] a tradition which was independent of Mark. At the same time there are also certain agreements between Luke and Mark against Matthew. These agreements prove that Luke was not really averse to conflating his sources, and that his version should not be taken as an unadulterated reproduction of Q.

Now Luke's main intention was obviously to use the double commandment as an introduction to the parable of the Good Samaritan. He does this by means of the catchword "neighbor."

In combining the two traditions Luke altered the Q text so as to produce—in comparison to Matthew—a variant from Q. But this is explicable from his use of Mark. First, he reformulates the question of the lawyer. Luke is not interested in the theoretical and speculative problem about which is the first and greatest commandment, but in the practical question concerning the moral law.[4] The new formulation then reads as follows: "What shall I do to inherit eternal life?" (Luke 10:25). These words prepare the way for Jesus' opening remark, "Do this, and you will live" (v. 28), and they are underscored by his final injunction, "Go, and do likewise" (v. 37). Now the original reformulation in v. 25 is reworded on the model of a formula which occurs at another place in Mark, viz., in the introduction of the rather similar pericope of the Rich Young Man: "What must I do to inherit eternal life?" (Mark 10:17).

In view of the examples just cited it appears to be Luke's procedure to use reminiscences from Mark's Gospel to weld together the traditions of the double commandment and the Good Samaritan. If that is correct, it will make it easier to explain another phenomenon, one which, as we have just seen, is often used as an argument for the originality of the Lucan version, viz., the fact that Luke ascribes the double commandment to the lawyer rather than to Jesus. There is already a trace of this in Mark 12:32-33, where the lawyer repeats the double commandment immediately after the pronouncement of Jesus. The reason for Luke's assignment of the double commandment to the lawyer rather than to Jesus is that for Luke the whole weight rests upon the story of the Good Samaritan, to which the double commandment is only an introduction. Its attribution in Luke to the lawyer is not original (despite the opinion of Beare and others) but Lucan redaction. This completely agrees with Luke's intention, which is to place all the emphasis on the injunction to follow the Good Samaritan's example, i.e., the dominical saying which forms the climax of the pericope (Luke 10:37). This intention is carried out by omitting Mark 12:29-30 and the Q parallel and by using Mark 12:32a-33 in its place. Possibly the saying about love being more important than cultic sacrifices gave Luke the idea of inserting here the story of the Good Samaritan.

Finally, there are three features in the Lucan version of the double commandment which are peculiar to the third evangelist. The first is the use of "And behold" as an introduction to the pericope (10:25). These words are often regarded as a Lucan Septuagintalism. If this is the case, we should assign it to the Lucan redaction. But T. Schramm has recently pointed out that Luke often introduces this formula into a Marcan passage from his special material.[5] If Schramm is right, this will be a Lucan introduction formulated in the style of special Luke.

The second characteristic is the phrase "stood up . . . saying" (10:25) where "stood up" is used pleonastically. The verb "to arise" or "to stand up" is one of Luke's favorite words, and it looks as though he has put the whole phrase in place of Mark's word "asked" which probably occurred in Q as well, as we shall see when we come to Matthew.

The third characteristic is much more problematical. In Luke both commandments are combined under a single imperative "You shall love" (10:27) without a connecting link as in Mark and Matthew. Is that a case of Lucan redaction or is the explanation to be found once more in the non-Marcan source? In favor of a pre-Lucan origin we might claim that the lawyer's question about the first and greatest commandment in Mark and Luke logically required a single commandment as the answer to the question "What shall I do?" On the other hand, it could also be argued that it was precisely the omission of the question, which is the first and greatest commandment, that led Luke to combine the two commandments. We will leave this problem for the moment and return to it after investigating the other two versions of the pericope.

In v. 28 Jesus accepts the double commandment as an adequate summary of the law. This explicit agreement has obviously become necessary as a result of the transference of the saying from Jesus to the lawyer. It must therefore be redactional.

Let us now turn to the Matthean version to see if we can find further pointers for the reconstruction of the non-Marcan source which both seemed to have used, Matthew as well as Luke. A slight yet not unimportant difference between Matthew and Mark is the inversion of the verb and subject at the beginning of the sentence. This might be merely a stylistic variant, but it is worth noticing that it contains a Semitism, and that is something which runs counter to Matthew's usual practice of improving Mark's Greek. That is why we prefer to ascribe this inversion to the non-Marcan source. Luke must have disturbed this sequence by the new introduction which he composed for the pericope in his own style (see above). Equally remarkable is the phrase "one from" which can hardly be ascribed to the Matthean redaction since it introduces a further Semitism. We presume therefore that the non-Marcan source read: "one from them, a lawyer" and not "a certain lawyer" (as in Luke). Luke must have dropped the Semitism in this verse. Moreover, Matthew has "great" instead of Mark's "first" while he combines both words in v. 38 "the great and the first." The Semitic use of the positive in place of the superlative seems to show once more that Matthew derived "great" from his non-Marcan source. The copula in the question of the lawyer (v. 36, contrasted with Mark 12:28) was omitted by Matthew, again a Semitic trait which can hardly be attributed to Matthean redaction. The introduction to Jesus' reply (v. 37: "and he said to him") is, however, typically Matthean[6] and must therefore be redactional.

Matthew mentions only three faculties, not four as in Mark and Luke. This agrees with Deut. 6:5 and seems to reproduce the non-Marcan source (cf. also Mark 12:33). Yet the third faculty in Matthew is the same as the fourth in Mark. Hence it appears likely that the non-Marcan tradition read "with all your strength." Thus it agrees with v. 27 in Luke (see above). The threefold formula (Matt. 22:37) is therefore a redactional combination of both Marcan and non-Marcan material. As regards the introduction to the second commandment, "the second is like it" (v. 39), what we have there is only a superficial alteration of the Marcan original; it can hardly be taken for a non-Marcan trait.[7] Matthew wants to underscore the way in which the love commandments complement each other. In any case the word "second" presupposes Mark's "first" and it is therefore unlikely that it stood in the other source. This source may then have combined the two commandments in the same way that Luke did.

Matt. 22:40 is a complete revision of Mark 12:31. Matthew is particularly fond of the expression, "the law and the prophets," which occurs only once in Q (Matt. 11:13=Luke 16:16). In addition the verb "hangs" or "depends" seems to represent a rabbinic term such as one might expect in the Matthean redaction.[8]

Now we are at last in the position to present a reconstruction: "And [there] asked one from them, [a] lawyer, tempting him: 'Master, which [is] the great commandment in the law?' And he said to him, 'You (singular) shall love [the] Lord your God in [with] all your heart and in all your soul and in all your strength, and your neighbor as yourself.' "

It will be noticed that this tradition contains four Semitisms:

The inversion of the verb and subject in the introduction, the phrase "one from," the omission of the copula in the question of the lawyer, and the usage of "in"="with" with the dative in the enumeration of the faculties. The list of the three faculties seems to suggest that it is the MT rather than the Septuagint which is being quoted. Hence it seems clear that this reconstruction must be fairly close to the earliest tradition. But is it actually the original tradition? That is the question.

In order to answer it we must turn to the Marcan version (Mark 12:28–34). Mark begins with a painfully overloaded introduction (v. 28), a sure sign of redactional expansion. The second and third parts of the sentence (v. 28b and c) are obvious Marcan composition, designed to tie in the pericope with the Marcan context, viz., a series of conflict stories. V. 12 refers to the two questions of the Pharisees (Mark 12:13–17) and the Sadducees (Mark 12:18–27). The more or less superfluous "came up" appears again in combination with "asked" in Mark's introduction to another pericope (10:2), and is a further redactional addition. Mark calls the questioner a "scribe," not a "lawyer," like Q. The word scribe is used in Hellenistic Greek for a lawyer in the wider sense (in Acts 13:35 it is used for a state official), whereas in Judaism it generally refers to an expert in the Torah. The Marcan "scribe" therefore appears to be of Palestinian origin and represents an earlier tradition than the "lawyer" in Q.[9]

Still more important is the fact that Mark does not know the word "tempting" or anything like it (Matt. 22:35=Luke 10:25). This changes the form-critical classification of the pericope. In the non-Marcan version it is a conflict story, but in Mark, where it is a reply to a friendly question, it is a scholastic dialogue. According to form-critical principles, conflict stories are secondary to scholastic dialogues.[10] This means that in this respect too the Marcan text would be more original than the other version. In the reconstruction of the earliest available form of the tradition we must therefore omit "tempting." We have already decided that the formulation of the question about "first and second" commandments (28c, 29a, 31a) is secondary. It must be ascribed to the Marcan redaction or at least to a special tradition following Mark. The use of the

Shemah as an introduction to the double commandment was obviously added for the sake of Gentile readers.[11] The construction "from" with the genitive in the list of faculties agrees with the Septuagint, and the addition of a fourth faculty, "mind," makes it quite clear for Hellenistic readers that God must be loved with the mind—which was already clearly stated in the Hebrew text by "your heart." Finally, vv. 32–34 must be a redactional addition of Mark. For as Bornkamm has shown, the preference of the moral law over the sacrificial cult presupposes a Hellenistic-Jewish rather than a rabbinic understanding of the law.[12] The insertion "understanding" (v. 33) corresponds to "mind" in v. 30, an indication that the passage has been adapted to a Hellenistic milieu.[13]

Only in the introduction then does the Marcan pericope help us to reconstruct the original text. The earliest attainable form is the non-Marcan form reconstructed above, but with the following change in the introduction: "And [there] asked him one from the scribes." The Semitisms and the suggestions of a Palestinian milieu in this reconstructed form permit us to take this pericope back to the earliest Aramaic speaking community.[14] But this does not prove the authenticity of the tradition. Strangely enough that is generally accepted without question, even by those who otherwise apply the strict Bultmannian criteria of authenticity.[15] Now it is certainly unlikely that the double commandment is a creation of the early post-Easter community[16] for, quite apart from our gospel pericope in its different versions, the post-Easter catechesis always quotes the single commandment to love the neighbor (Gal. 5:14; Rom. 13:9; Jas. 2:8; also Matt. 19:19), a tendency which can be shown to go back to rabbinic sources.[17] Thus the double commandment is handed down in a different form from that in which it appears in early Christian catechesis. But much more problematic is its relationship to Judaism. The double commandment, as is well known, appears neither in the rabbinic writings nor in Qumran, to say nothing of the apocalyptic. But it does appear in several places in the Testaments of the Twelve Patriarchs. Some of these, like the logion of Jesus, clearly follow Deut. 6:5 and Lev. 19:18. I quote the most important of these passages. First, Test. Issachar 5:2, "But love the Lord and your neighbor." Here both commandments are combined in a single imperative—as in Luke and in our reconstruction of the non-Marcan version. A second place which displays this feature reflects the threefold listing of the faculties as in Deut. 6:5, but transfers them to the second commandment: "I loved the Lord, likewise every man with all my heart" (Test. Iss. 7:6).

Particularly noticeable here is the way in which the commandment to love the neighbor is generalized. This parallels the expansion of it in the Sermon on the Mount to include the neighbor and the enemy, i.e., the non-Israelite. A third reference to the double commandment appears in Test. Dan 5:3, "Love the Lord . . . . And one another with a true heart." Even if this text cannot be interpreted in such a general human sense as the reference in Test. Issachar 7:6, yet it combines both commandments in a single imperative and mentions once more the faculties, which shows quite clearly that the author had Deut. 6:5 in mind. The use of "in" (with) with the dative will be discussed later (see below).

J. Becker proposed, in opposition to the dominant trend since Charles, that the Testaments are of Hellenistic–Jewish origin.[18] This holds also for the basic document behind the Testaments in which the parallels to the double commandment of love mentioned above occur. Furthermore, Becker cites alleged parallels to the double commandment from unquestionably Hellenistic-Jewish literature in order to show the double commandment of love stems from Hellenistic Judaism. To prove this, he cites a series of parallels. It is worth while quoting these parallels in full so as to have them before us.

The first passage is Aristeas 229. It reads as follows:

"What is of like value with beauty?" And he said, "Piety, for piety is the first degree of beauty; its power is love" (Tr. Hadas). This is not a real parallel because it does not mention specifically the love of neighbor. It must also be noted that Aristeas, instead of speaking directly of the love of God, introduces the typically Hellenistic concept of "piety." This expression also occurs in four passages from Philo to which Becker refers, and is in each case related to the expression "humanity," another typically Hellenistic expression for the love of neighbor.

The first passage in Philo occurs in *On the Virtues* 51. There we read:

"The next subject to be examined is humanity, the virtue closest to piety, its sister and its twin."

It is to be noted that this statement does not refer to the Torah, still less to a passage like Deut. 6:5 or Lev. 19:6.

The second passage is to be found in the same book, *On the Virtues* 95:

"The ornament of those queens of the virtues, piety and humanity" (Loeb Tr.).

This passage occurs in the context of a discussion of the original principle lying behind the specific injunctions of the Torah. Hence the formula has the same meaning and performs the same function as the double commandment in the synoptic tradition. But here again there is no direct quotation, or combination of the two commandments from Deuteronomy and Leviticus. The verb "honor" comes close to a citation but the biblical echo is immediately destroyed by "the divine."

The third passage is *The Special Laws* II 63, where we read:

"But among the vast number of particular truths and principles there studied, there stand out practically high above the others two heads: one of duty to God as shown by piety and holiness, one of duty to men as shown by humanity and justice" (Loeb Tr.).

The mention of "truths and principles" makes it crystal clear that Philo considers the Hellenistic categories "piety and humanity" as equivalents to the first and second part of the double commandment, and that is why he also adds "justice." But as above this is not directly related to Deuteronomy or Leviticus.

The last passage comes from *On Abraham* 208. There we read:

"For the nature which is pious is also kindly, and the same person will exhibit both qualities, holiness to God and justice to men" (Loeb Tr.)

Here again we have the same four categories, piety/humanity and holiness/justice, while this passage again makes no direct reference to the Torah. Instead, the four qualities are regarded, two for God and two for man, as the basic principle of natural law. But this fact must not be overestimated for it is quite clear that Philo regards the general principles of the Mosaic Torah as an expression of natural law. On the whole we can agree with Dieter Georgi when he says: "Here the double commandment is clearly understood as the summary of the law, and that also means that it is the key to the exposition of the law and to the liturgy of the synagogue."[19] It must however be emphasized that Philo never quotes the double commandment verbatim. All he does is summarize its content in Stoic categories.[20]

If Georgi is right and if, as Becker argues, the basis of the Testaments is Hellenistic–Jewish rather than Palestinian–Jewish, one is justified in arguing that the double commandment came into early Christianity originally via Hellenistic Judaism as Burchard also thinks.[21] In this case the question of authenticity has been answered in the negative.

But is this opinion justified? There is a decisive difference between the passages from Aristeas and Philo on the one hand and the material from the Testaments and the synoptics on the other. This is, as we have already noted, that the former constantly express the double commandment of love in Stoic terminology, whereas the latter cite Deuteronomy and Leviticus verbatim or allude to them indirectly. Therefore it is clear that we are dealing here with a very different world of thought. There can be no doubt that the desire to summarize the Torah under two basic principles was, so to speak, in the air throughout the Hellenistic world in Palestine as well as outside of it. But it is most unlikely that the explicit use of the double commandment in the Testaments and in the synoptics is derived from Hellenistic Judaism. For the basic idea was expressed in very different ways in Palestine and outside of it.

Apart from this, Becker's opinion that the original basis of the Testaments was Hellenistic is by no means proved, let alone universally accepted. It is worthwhile emphasizing that Test. Dan 5:3 uses the construction "in" (with) with the dative and explicitly mentions the faculties with which we are to love God or the neighbor respectively. This seems to point to the possibility of a Semitic origin. Moreover the discovery of an Aramaic fragment of the Testament of Levi in Cave 4 at Qumran proves that the beginnings of the Testament literature must be sought in Palestine rather than in Hellenistic Judaism. But this is not to say that we insist on a rigorous separation of these two types of Judaism. The discoveries at Qumran have, as a matter of fact, thrown considerable doubt on such distinctions. It becomes increasingly clear that all forms of Palestinian Judaism, including Pharisaism, were in varying degrees receptive to Hellenistic influences. We have found an example of this in the attempt to summarize the Torah in one or two basic commandments.[22]

Such Hellenistic influences could have affected Jesus as well as the earliest Aramaic speaking church, even in Palestine. This possibility would solve the apparent conflict between the criteria of language and milieu on the one hand and the criterion of dissimilarity on the other. But this raises the question whether it was Jesus himself or the earliest Palestinian community that introduced the double commandment of love into the Christian tradition. Which of the parties would have been more susceptible to the type of Judaism represented in the basic document behind the Testament of the Twelve Patriarchs? Here we must fall back on the criterion of coherence. It is generally accepted that the focal point of Jesus' message was the inbreaking of the kingdom of God. It is clear that the post-Easter community was concerned to associate the love commandment with this eschatological proclamation: "You are not far from the kingdom of God" (Mark 12:34); "What shall I do to inherit eternal life?" (Luke 10:25).

The original text of the double commandment, as we have reconstructed it above, makes no claim to such an association. This raises for us a highly interesting possibility. In the Testaments the double commandment is associated with wisdom, cf. e.g., Test. Naphtali, 8:9–10:

"So then, there are two commandments; and unless they are done in due order, they bring very great sin upon man. Be ye therefore

wise in God, my children, and *prudent,* understanding the order
of his commandments, and the laws of every word, that the Lord
may love you."

The same association occurs in Test. Levi 13:7:

"Get wisdom in the fear of God with diligence."

If then the double commandment of love has affinities with the
Hellenized wisdom tradition and was already known in first
century Palestine, and if too it is found in the Jesus tradition,
could it not be that the double commandment is rooted in the
same wisdom tradition? That would suggest that there were two
sides in the thought world of Jesus, the one apocalyptic and the
other derived from the wisdom tradition.

In his use of apocalyptic, Jesus implicitly identifies himself in
his earthly ministry with the heavenly Son of man. In similar
fashion we may conclude that his use of the double commandment
of love involved an implicit claim to be the spokesman of the
wisdom tradition.

Jesus appears on earth as the representative of the divine wisdom. After Easter this wisdom Christology becomes explicit. It
finds its earliest expression in the sayings source (Q)[23] and its
climax in the Johannine prologue.

NOTES

1. See e.g., F. W. Beare, *The Earliest Records of Jesus* (Oxford, 1962), 159; V. Taylor, *The Gospel According to St. Mark* (New York, ²1966), 484.

2. Beare, *ibid.* This argument was also expressed by my late colleague, Professor C. C. Richardson, in a letter to me dated December 29, 1971.

3. In his letter of December 29 (see above, note 2), Professor Richardson used this as an argument for the originality of a form in which there was only one commandment, viz., the command to love God, and not two (from the viewpoint of the lawyer). This argument has some importance, but it does not prove that the second commandment is unauthentic, assuming that the two were combined from the outset.

4. This was discussed by A. Plummer, *The Gospel According to St. Luke,* (Edinburgh, 1922), 293. T. Schramm, *Der Markus-Stoff bei Lukas* (Cambridge, 1971), 48 finds in Luke 3:10–14; 6:46ff.; 8:21; Acts 2:37 (16:30); 22:10 a similar concern in the Lucan redaction for the practical as opposed to the theological and speculative.

5. Schramm, *op. cit.,* 91–92.

6. Matthew has "said" 13 or 15 times (depending on the text at Matthew 19:18, 21), Mark six times, and Luke seven times. In the second half of Acts it appears 11 times, which shows that Luke did not object to the word. It is therefore hardly to be supposed that he intentionally eliminated it from his source.

7. G. Strecker, *Der Weg der Gerechtigkeit* (Göttingen, ³1971), 25–26, agrees that the Matthean version is a combination of Mark and Q. But because he does not wish to postulate a knowledge of the Massoretic text by Matthew he thinks that the threefold formula must be traced back to the LXX. That is basically possible: but if the threefold form was already present in Q one could postulate a knowledge of the Massoretic text for the tradition that lies behind it. I am not claiming that Matthew had a direct knowledge of the Massoretic text.

8. See also A. Schlatter, *Der Evangelist Matthäus* (Stuttgart,

[3]1948) *ad loc.* According to R. Bultmann, *The History of the Synoptic Tradition* (Oxford, 1972), 90, Matt. 22:40 is an addition.

9. Cf. G. Bornkamm, "Das Doppelgebot der Liebe," in E. Dinkler (ed.) *Neutestamentliche Studien für Rudolf Bultmann* (Berlin, 1954), 85–93, reprinted in *Geschichte und Glaube I, Gesammelte Aufsätze III* (Munich, 1968), 37–45 (page quotations follow the reprint). He is followed by Christoph Burchard, "Das Doppelgebot der Liebe in der frühen christlichen Überlieferung" in *Der Ruf Jesu und die Antwort der Gemeinde* (J. Jeremias Festschrift; Göttingen, 1970), 39–62, esp. 51.

10. R. Bultmann, *Synoptische Tradition,* 39; G. Bornkamm, "Doppelgebot," 37: a classical instance of the scholastic dialogue.

11. G. Bornkamm, "Doppelgebot," 39. He observes that Mark —like Diaspora Judaism—regards the Shemah as the supreme commandment. He concludes with the observation that "The use of the 'monotheistic' credo of Deut. 6:4 points clearly to Hellenistic Jewish theology" (p. 40).

12. Bornkamm, *op. cit.,* 41, note 7, quotes Pseudo-Aristeas 234 as an example of Hellenistic–Jewish critique of the sacrificial cultus.

13. Bornkamm, "Doppelgebot," 40. He adds that " 'truly' is good Greek."

14. Contra Burchard, *ibid.* In his opinion, both the Matthean and Lucan versions are redactional alterations of the Marcan text. The latter he considers the oldest, though a Hellenistic–Jewish version. Burchard ignores the possibility of Semitisms and a Palestinian cultural milieu in the Matthean and Lucan variations from Mark and therefore sees no hints of a pre-Hellenistic tradition.

15. E.g., Bornkamm, "Doppelgebot," 45, who opts for the priority of Luke's version, and E. Jüngel, *Paulus und Jesus* (Tübingen, 1962), 169–70, who considers the Marcan version older, despite the many signs of Hellenistic influence which make it unlikely that the pericope in its present form is authentic to Jesus himself.

16. The earliest references to the double commandment outside the gospels appear first in the second century: *Didache* 1:2a; Justin, *Dialogue* 93:3. Here the knowledge of the synoptic tradition is presupposed (even if not necessarily of the written gospels). See H. Köster, *Synoptische Überlieferungen bei den apostolischen Vätern* (Berlin, 1957), 170–72.

17. (Strack-) Billerbeck I, 907 quotes the well-known sayings of Hillel and Akiba.

18. J. Becker, *Untersuchungen zur Entstehungsgeschichte der Testamente der Zwölf Patriarchen* (Leiden, 1970), 377–401. For a report on Becker's work see H. D. Slingerland, *The Testaments of the Twelve Patriarchs: A Critical History of Research* (SBLMS 21; Missoula, 1977), 79–82.

19. D. Georgi, *Die Gegner des Paulus im 2. Korintherbrief* (Neukirchen-Vluyn, 1964), 88, note 3.

20. Becker, *Untersuchungen,* 39c.

21. Burchard mentions the same passage which we have quoted and concludes: "The double commandment of love as a summary of the divine will must be a legacy from Hellenistic Judaism, to which early Christianity owes much besides that which comes under the heading of 'love' " ("Liebesgebot," 57).

22. It is noticeable that the idea of the double commandment also appears in Jub. 20:2: "And he commanded them that they should observe the way of the Lord; that they should work righteousness, and love each his neighbor" (Tr. Charles). Fragments of this book were also found at Qumran, and this document exhibits clear parallels with the Qumran literature in many aspects. Although we cannot agree with R. Marcus in his article "The Qumran Scrolls and Early Judaism," *Biblical Research* I, (1956), 9–11, where he argues for an Essene source for Jubilees, it is clear that the ideas of Jubilees were not unknown to sectarian Judaism in New Testament times.

23. See F. Christ, *Jesus Sophia* (Zürich, 1970). This work decides rather too easily in favor of the authenticity of five Q sayings investigated (the justification saying, the cry of jubilation, the Savior's call, the wisdom saying, and the Jerusalem saying). We

would prefer to regard these sayings as formations of the post-Easter community, which developed an explicit wisdom Christology on the basis of the traditions of Jesus as a teacher of wisdom. For further discussion of the wisdom Christology see J. M. Robinson and H. Koester, *Trajectories Through Early Christianity* (Philadelphia, 1971), 71–113, 232–68.

CHRISTOPH BURCHARD

The Theme of
the Sermon on the Mount

1.

It is Matthew, not Jesus, who is the author of the Sermon on the Mount. True, Matthew constructed it from texts which had been transmitted to him as sayings of Jesus. In the eyes of the first evangelist the original disciples regarded themselves to be bound to the words of the *earthly* Jesus, and to nothing else. Matthew has Jesus emphasize this point quite early in the Sermon, and the resurrected Lord corroborates it.[1] Despite that, the Sermon on the Mount is not a mine where authentic sayings of Jesus can be dug up like pure gold, all in the day's work, and, if possible, in a representative selection. Such a hope has fostered interest in the Sermon both within the church and outside it down to this very day,[2] and even makes itself felt in the works of New Testament scholars. However, the conditions under which the pre-gospel tradition was transmitted here are not basically different from those governing the four other discourses in Matthew[3] and the synoptic tradition as a whole.[4] Only a lengthy and laborious methodological road can lead us to the historical Jesus, as Ferdinand Hahn has recently shown, and as Dieter Lührmann has demonstrated in such exemplary fashion.[5] Sooner or later we are bound to realize that Matthew is the author of the Sermon in its finished form and the last to give shape to its constituent parts.

My concern in this essay is with the factors that determined the composition of Matt. 5:3–7:27, the longest unbroken discourse of Jesus in the synoptics. Redaction criticism should have made them clear. But although it has been very much concerned with the component parts of the Sermon, especially with the fifth chapter, such criticism has not paid sufficient attention to the composition as a whole. At any rate, there is room for further reflection.[6]

2.

In 4:17 we have a programmatic statement about the preaching of Jesus. This verse introduces a new section of the Gospel.[7] It begins with the call of the first disciples in 4:18–22 and with the summary of Jesus' ministry in word and deed in 4:23–25. Then in 5:1–7:29 there follows the Sermon on the Mount which constitutes the first major episode in the ministry. The Sermon is followed by a string of (mainly) miracle stories in 8:1–9:34 and by the summary in 9:35, which repeats 4:23 almost word for word. Even if the usual designation of the two summaries as a framework for chaps. 5–9 is not quite correct, it is clear that we ought to place a caesura at 9:35. For the second summary is not so much a conclusion to the preceding section as an introduction to the disciples' mission. In spite of this, the repetition shows that the material from 4:23–25 onward should be regarded as a unity. This is especially true since Matthew regards the Sermon on the Mount and the narratives that follow as sub-sections to the Gospel, though he clearly does not wish to separate them (8:1).[8] It is usual nowadays to take 4:23–25 (9:35) and 5:1–9:34 as the statement of a theme and its execution. The Sermon and the narratives that follow it develop and interpret the teaching and the miraculous activity of Jesus, which the summary only mentions by title. In this way they show who Jesus is, "The Messiah of the word" and "the Messiah of deed."[9] Thus the Sermon corresponds to the teaching and preaching of 4:23 (9:35), to one or the other of the two verses. This I cannot accept.

Take first 4:23 (9:35). There is no reason whatever to draw a distinction between teaching and preaching—the one taking place in the synagogue, the other where possible out of doors.[10] Matthew characterizes the ministry of Jesus through the word by the use of these two terms. Often he wishes to stress some particular aspect, but he can also use them synonymously.[11] When he speaks of "teaching in their synagogues" he probably means no more than sabbath preaching with the gospel of the kingdom as its theme. This sounds rather technical and it is tempting to interpret it by taking a cross section of Matthew's use of the term and of the way it had been used in the pre-Matthean tradition.[12] But the phrase, which occurs elsewhere in Matthew only at 24:14 and nowhere else in early Christian literature, is not so stereotyped to allow us to ignore the context in which it occurs. According to 4:17, Jesus began to preach repentance because the kingdom was near at hand. Six verses later, after the call of the first disciples, which does nothing to change the theme, the phrase, "the gospel of the kingdom" can hardly mean anything else than the carrying out of 4:17. Our point is corroborated by 9:35ff. In the missionary charge of 10:5–42, which 9:35ff. introduces, Jesus orders his disciples to perform the same things which he is doing in 9:35. In particular, 10:5b–8a takes up 9:35–36 again, though in the reverse order. Thus the term "the gospel of the kingdom" is explained by 10:7. The kingdom of heaven is at hand. The proclamation of this message draws the multitudes together according to 4:25. These multitudes vary in Matthew between being interested and sympathetic, at least up to the time of the passion.[13] The word "followed" hints at that here.

The situation is different with 5:1–7:29. According to 5:1–2, Jesus, seeing the crowds, goes up on a mountain and teaches his disciples. It looks as though he is turning his back on the multitude in contrast to 9:36, where the same phrase, "saw the crowds" introduces a movement toward them (although there is no discourse here). Yet in a way the situation is similar to what we have in 8:18 (cf. 13:36). The mountain here, as later in 14:23; 15:29; 17:1,9; 28:16, is the place of special communication with God, suspended as it were between heaven and earth. And in any case, it is to be distinguished from "their synagogues."[14]

In Matthew the disciples are mainly the Twelve, even if not exclusively so. They do not form a unique circle of apostles as is the case in Luke; rather they stand for all Jesus' disciples who have set out on the path of discipleship in a way quite different from the multitudes.[15] It is they who are addressed in the Sermon on the Mount, as the constant repetition of "your Father in heaven" shows,[16] and—what is not the same thing—the Sermon applies to them, too. There is not a word about repentance or about the imminence of the kingdom. Instead we have instructions for those who have received the gospel of the kingdom and who are now living in the interval before the end, as we shall presently try to show. The scenic remark at the conclusion of the Sermon at 7:28–29 would seem at first sight to contradict this point. The multitudes are amazed because Jesus speaks with a greater authority than their scribes. Anyone who subsumes the Sermon on the Mount under 4:23–25 finds Matthew's intention logically here, not in 5:1–2. But read in the sense suggested above, the passage can only mean that the Sermon is not a piece of esoteric teaching. To this extent, though only to this extent, it is intended for everyone, just as everyone is invited to discipleship.[17]

This means that for Matthew the Sermon on the Mount does not express "the gospel of the kingdom" (4:23; 9:35) or a "general summary of Jesus' teaching."[18] What is it then?

3.

One way of answering this question is to analyze the structure of the Sermon on the Mount. By structure we do not mean the usual summary of the themes treated, a sort of list of contents, but a systematic demonstration of the way in which it is articulated, describing how its constituent parts are related to one another, with the major sections formulated as propositions. Given the prevailing views of Matthew's method of composition,[19] such a task ought not to be too difficult, especially since the Sermon provides its own headings for some of the longer sections.[20] Of course, we should not look for anything as formal as the old-fashioned outlines for essays or sermons, if only because Matthew is working with materials which were shaped almost in their entirety before him, and to some extent were already grouped together.

It is quite easy to divide up the Sermon on the Mount according to its form or content into the smallest units of sense and sometimes these units can be grouped together to form larger sections. Translations of the Bible, synopses, and commentaries do this as a matter of course, marking their divisions with headings, sometimes at all three levels.[21] While there are a few problems regarding the division of the sections, the real difficulty is how to relate the sections to the Sermon as a whole, especially at the uppermost level. Let me start, as so many have done before me, with the fact that Matthew himself marks off what looks like the body of the Sermon on the Mount with his generalizing remarks about the law and the prophets in 5:17 and 7:12, thus indicating the subject matter of the central core. This makes 5:3–16 serve as an introduction and 7:13–27 as a postscript. This does not mean, however, that these sections are subordinated to the main part, and we had better refrain from referring to them that way. Much depends on the way we understand the introduction.

4.

The introduction to the Sermon on the Mount begins with the beatitudes (5:3–12).[22] There can be no doubt that Matthew understands them in a spiritualizing and ethical sense.[23] They do not enjoin poverty as such, but poverty "in spirit," whatever that means exactly. Such poverty is not a condition a person is living in when he is encountered by the gospel, but a condition he must fulfill. The beatitudes are indirect injunctions, not virtues to be pursued as occasion arises. Rather, they suggest the lineaments of an overall attitude to life. That is why the apodoses are virtually synonymous as v. 10, created by Matthew as an echo of v. 3b, shows.[24] Thus it is no wonder that we have some difficulty in deciding what is distinctive about each of the protases. Only one thing is certain. They do not refer exclusively to actions.[25] The same v. 10 also shows what the beatitudes are all about. It takes up the substance of vv. 11–12[26] into the series of beatitudes formulated in the third person plural. Thus vv. 11–12 interpret v. 10. Evidently in spite of the traditional formulation, Matthew hears Jesus from v. 3 on speaking not of just anyone who fulfills his injunctions, but quite specifically of the disciples. This was already true for Q as well as for Luke. The protases of the Matthean beatitudes do not lay down stipulations for conversion, but represent *notae ecclesiae*.[27]

But this does not mean that the prelude to the Sermon, (5:3–12) announces the requirements of the Christian life. Nor, assuming that the disciples are the subject, does it simply drive home those requirements once more. If that were the case, they would have been incorporated in one form or another into the body of the Sermon. The key words in the protases hardly ever come up again, while the key words in the body of the Sermon do not occur in the introduction.[28] This is not the case, however, with the kingdom and the question of rewards which appear in the apotases. It is not the injunctions as such that are driven home, but the reasons for them which are expressed in the apodoses. The protases are addressed to the disciples as men who are poor in spirit, who hunger after righteousness, and who are sometimes persecuted—which is what Christians are suffering by Matthew's time. These terms might well represent what Matthew's community actually called themselves, like the term "little ones."[29] The apodoses remind them of the reward which is attached to those conditions in the kingdom of God. In other words, the beatitudes are not "conditions of entrance" or "tables of eschatological virtues," or anything of the kind,[30] although they could be that. Rather, they are consoling reminders of the promise, "rejoice and be glad."[31]

The group of sayings in 5:13–16[32] follows on well since they continue the second person plural introduced for the first time in v. 11, and as far as the form is concerned, they move in the same way from the indicative to the imperative. But the scene shifts from heaven (v. 12) to earth (v. 13), i.e., from the future kingdom to the interim before it comes, and from the hopes people quite rightly cherish for themselves and the group to which they belong to service for others. That, too, is a source of comfort. The modest life-style of the disciples makes sense, not only in view of what lies ahead, but also at the present time. Yet the accent has shifted from the gift to the task. There is a hint of this, though a negative one, in the judgment threatened in v. 13b, which appears immediately with the first use of the plural "you."[33] The same thing is stated positively in v. 16, which interprets the preceding sayings. "Earth" and "world" mean the whole human race, and to be the salt of the earth and the light of the world means to let them see your good works so that they may glorify God.[34]

If 5:3–16 is the introduction to the Sermon we shall need a bridge to connect it with what follows. Such a bridge is not easy to find and the commentators have not seriously tried to find one. With the introduction of the first person singular and the reference to the law and the prophets, the Sermon appears to take quite a new turn. True, the argumentative "Think not" at the beginning of v. 17 takes for granted that there is some point of contact. But the commentators generally look for such a point outside the literary context in the opposition Matthew's community had to face. That there was such opposition may be perfectly true. But 5:17ff. is attached more closely to the preceding text than would seem to be the case at first glance. It is well known that 5:16 is original neither in wording nor content, but comes from a tradition reaching back to Judaism.[35] The more suggestive parallel, not only for 5:16 but for everything that follows, is to be found in Rom. 2:17ff., Paul's polemic against Hellenistic Judaism and its slogans. For Hellenistic Judaism sought to be "the light to those who are in darkness," the teachers of the human race. It knows "[God's] will" and possesses "the embodiment of the knowledge and truth of God." It "teaches" the ten commandments to others but does not keep them itself. In this way it contributes to the "blaspheming of God among the Gentiles."[36] It would seem that Matthew is alluding to a string of items similar to those quoted by Paul. Matthew is not writing in a polemical vein but taking them up in a Christian sense, and only after that giving them a polemical slant. This is the clue to the way his thought moves from 5:13–16 to 5:17ff.[37]

This helps us in the first place to understand v. 16. It is no accident that Matthew applies the image of light here, and only with a parenetic intention. This shows that he is not concerned with some particular aspect of Christian behavior, but with Christian behavior as a whole. That is why "good works" means good in a general ethical sense, not in the technical sense of rabbinic literature.[38] The men referred to are not men in general, but non-

Christians. They are to be won over to faith in God. The Sermon on the Mount is not in the least bit concerned with the state or any other kind of organization. The whole passage describes the raison d'être of the disciples in the world, and refers to the disciples as a whole, not to a group with some special commission.[39] Thus the commentators are quite right when they connect this passage and Matt. 28:16–20.[40] And we should probably connect it with 4:19 as well.[41] Most important, however, this means that in 5:17ff. we are not unprepared for the requirements of the law and the prophets, since that is what 5:16 is driving at. It tells us what the light is which the disciples are to show before mankind. And it is mankind as a whole that the Sermon on the Mount has constantly in view.

If we are right, then 5:3–16 serves as a kind of heading to the body of the Sermon on the Mount (5:17–7:12). It is not exactly a prelude but a summary of the contents. 5:16 is, as it were, the theme of the Sermon. What follows is the development of that theme. This is how the disciples must behave quite concretely if they are to be the light of the world. How is all this carried out?

5.

The body of the Sermon begins with a fundamental declaration about the law and the prophets (5:17–20).[42] From a formal point of view, these verses constitute a single block of material.[43] The basic law of justice (v. 17) is followed by the reason for it in eschatology (v. 18). Then we have two antithetical statements to elucidate that law (v. 19), followed by an application of it to the current situation (v. 20). Between vv. 16 and 19 the laconic expressions "abolish" and "fulfill" in v. 17 hardly refer to fulfillment in the salvation-historical sense, as in the case of Matthew's fulfillment quotations. It means the same thing as "relaxing and teaching" or "doing and teaching" the commandments as they are laid down in the law and the prophets (v. 19).[44] To do and to teach even the least of these commandments[45] is an integral part of Jesus' mission.[46] For they continue in force right up to the End (v. 18).[47] One's place in the kingdom is decided by whether one keeps them or not (v. 19). If v. 20 is a concrete application of the preceding injunction, then "righteousness," i.e., the disciples' fulfillment of the commandments,[48] can only mean "doing and teaching" even the least of them. Such righteousness far exceeds the righteousness of the scribes and Pharisees, because *they* only "relax" the commandments. Only in this way does v. 20 represent an interruption in the train of thought. Those who relax the commandments will find no place in the kingdom. 5:17–20 says nothing about any expansion of the application of the Old Testament commandments on the part of Jesus. Rather, he re-interprets them radically in contrast with the tendencies to relax them which Matthew sees not only among the Christian antinomians,[49] but also in his Jewish contemporaries.[50]

Now Matt. 5:20 leads into the antitheses in 5:21–48.[51] It is necessary for us to demonstrate that as Matthew sees it, the antitheses are not directed against the commandments of the Old Testament, but against "relaxing" them. Then we need to show how they are "done and taught." This is not impossible.

In the first place, only one of the actual theses within the antitheses occurs word for word in the Old Testament, and thus clearly represents a definite though doubly attested statement. This occurs in 5:27, which comes from Exod. 20:13 with a parallel in Deut. 5:17. Another thesis has only one "and" too many. This is 5:38 which is just a fragment of a complete statement, and has three possible sources which though similar are not identical, viz., Exod. 21:24; Deut. 19:21; and Lev. 24:20. All the other theses have no parallel either in wording or in meaning to any passage in the Old Testament. On the other hand, they do not occur in the Halacha, but have some foundation in the Old Testament itself. 5:21 is a commandment (Exod. 20:15 and Deut. 5:18); 5:43 is an injunction which is not quite complete. It occurs in Lev. 19:18, but here it is without the phrase "as yourself." The last two both have an addition which is not found in the Old Testament. 5:31 and 5:33 do not occur anywhere in the Old Testament, not even approximately (cf. Deut. 24:1 and Lev. 19:12). This form, curiously neglected in the literature,[52] indicates that Matthew, whose familiarity with the Old Testament has never been called into question, did not regard the theses as Old Testament quotations, but rather

as expressions of the "righteousness of the scribes and Pharisees."
The introductory formula, "it was said," does not contradict the
point we are making. It cannot be a divine passive and it would
be wrong to take it as such. If in any way it invokes the divine
authority, it does so only in the consciousness of the author of
these formulae. And it is not the scribes of the day who are referred to. "The ancients" belong to earlier generations.[53] This is
not a new idea, but those who hold this view generally think that
Matthew is really concerned with the commandments that underlie
the theses.[54] This opinion is virtually unanimous today: the antitheses in Matthew's view are alterations of the Old Testament
commandments. Partly they intensify them, and partly they replace
them.[55] But is this really so?

In the first antithesis, 5:21–26, the second clause in the thesis
does not refer, as is commonly stated in summary fashion, to the
relevant punishments laid down in the Old Testament, which
Matthew misquotes with an almost tautological turn of phrase.
Rather, it limits the application of the fifth commandment to
"killing," no more and no less. *Per contra,* the antithesis presumes
cases which *a fortiori* fall under the commandment. In other words,
it intensifies the commandment, but does not radicalize it. In fact,
the commandment is not really quoted at all. What this antithesis
does is to remove all restrictions to its application.[56] The phrase
"but I say unto you" does not mean that the speaker is expounding
the law in a different sense from current opinion (though that is a
formal possibility).[57] Nor is he a lawgiver who transcends Moses
and corrects him from an eschatological perspective. Rather, his
mission is "to do and to teach" the will of God as it is written in
the law and the prophets in a quite final way.[58]

The second antithesis, 5:27–30, may be interpreted in a similar
way to the first, despite the fact that its thesis cites the sixth commandment in a pure form.[59] The sixth antithesis, 5:43–47, is also
open to a similar interpretation. The second half of the thesis
which prescribes limits to the commandment of love is abrogated.
This of course assumes that Matthew has already understood the
"neighbor" in a no longer restricted sense. In the third, fourth, and
fifth antitheses, 5:31f., 33–37, and 38–42, the theses should be

regarded as "relaxations," although the relevant commandment is not directly quoted. In the case of 5:31 this is indicated by the brief introduction, "it was also said," the only instance without "you have heard that," and the fresh start at 5:33 with the full introduction, the only instance of this apart from the first one. Evidently the third antithesis follows closely upon the preceding one, and there is still an echo of the sixth commandment from 5:27.[60] No such possibility can be entertained for 5:33 and 5:38. If any particular commandment is in mind here, which one is it? It can hardly be one of the commandments in the decalogue, e.g., from the second table.[61] Do not the commandments stand at the beginning of the anti-theses, "do not swear at all" (5:34) and "do not resist evil" (5:39)?[62] Only these two anti-theses counter the thesis with a fundamental principle: the first three cases with "every one who" + a verb, the last case in the imperative, which does not include everyone. The two fundamental principles could not stand in the theses because in these two cases the theses not merely restrict one of the commandments but actually abrogate it.

Although as Matthew sees it, the theses represent Jewish scribal tradition, this does not mean that they are actually taken over from Judaism. For there are closer parallels to the anti-theses than to the theses, and only a few of them will fit into a definitely Jewish milieu.[63] Both in their entirety and in each single instance they are Christian formations, and have actually been composed *ad hoc* to refute the antitheses.[64] How they actually came into being is a question which can only be answered in each individual case.[65]

If all this is true, it calls for a fresh approach to several questions. What interpretation of the law do the antitheses imply? How did Matthew understand them as a whole? What is their background? What opponents are they directed against? Of the commandments which Matthew has reconstructed in 5:21–48 from the law and the prophets, only the first two and the last one actually come from the Old Testament. If we connect 5:31 with Gen. 1:27 and 2:24 as is done in Matt. 19:4–5, one further injunction from the Old Testament may be added to the list, though it does not actually occur there in the form of a commandment. It expresses "the will of my Father in heaven" (Matt. 7:21), the fulfillment of which, i.e., the perfect righteousness, is rewarded by admission to the kingdom. We do not have here a long list of basic principles, some of which, like the decalogue and the commandment of love, are given classic formulation in the Old Testament, and the other prescriptions not. Rather, they serve as headings for specific ethical prescriptions from various spheres of life. In Matt. 5:23–24, they include the proper mode of behavior in relation to the sacrificial cultus. In this way Matthew is able to take 5:18–19 seriously. Yet they can be summarized once more in a supreme maxim as in 5:48 (be perfect as God is perfect) or in substance at 7:12 (the golden rule, which again does not occur anywhere in the Old Testament). A further such summary occurs outside of the Sermon on the Mount, at 22:37–40 (the double commandment of love).[66] All this is quite different from the way the rabbis present it and suggests quite a different understanding of the law, not simply a Christian variant of the rabbinic teaching.[67] In my opinion it would be more worthwhile to trace the references to the Wisdom tradition as roots.[68] The milieu should be sought preferably in the diaspora.[69] In spite of that, Matthew's Jewish opponents, if he had any,[70] should be looked for in the main in Judaism as it was reorganized on Pharisaic principles after A.D. 70. But this does not mean that Matthew himself was part of that reorganization. Even that fact is not so obvious as it is usually thought to be.[71]

In any case, 5:17–20 must be read as a preamble to the antitheses, not to the body of the Sermon on the Mount as a whole.[72] Only 5:17–48 is concerned with the contrast between relaxing and fulfilling the law and with the controversy with the scribes and Pharisees.[73] Of course, when the preamble talks about "the law and the prophets" and "righteousness," it is introducing terms which will later provide a framework for the materials incorporated. But as we shall seek to show, this does not mean that 5:17–20 is meant as a title for the rest of the Sermon.

The next section consists of 6:1–18.[74] This passage is divided into three sections, but in form and substance they constitute a unity. There is no need to prove this point again. 6:1, which certainly comes from Matthew's hand, serves as a guiding principle, and at the same time provides a connecting link with 5:17–48. The second section shows what "your righteousness" is. It fleshes out the kind of behavior described in the antitheses. Almsgiving, prayer, and fasting are not for Matthew additional injunctions to those he has given already. They do not represent some new area of piety he has not yet covered, still less are they some sort of narrow religious practice demanded by God. As a matter of fact, Matthew has mentioned them already (cf. 5:42, 44), although he did not specifically mention fasting. He is not making Jesus require such practices, but rather he sets out a particular way of doing them if they are done at all. Disregarding the catchword "righteousness," 6:1c links the following section to 5:16. In v. 2 we have "that they may be praised by men" instead of "that they may be seen by men" as in vv. 5 and 16, which is certainly more primitive and serves to underscore our point. "Men" here means non-Christians, as in 5:16.

Matthew hardly means that almsgiving, prayer, and fasting are not works that show light in the sense of 5:16 (5:42 enjoins almsgiving and 5:44 prayer). What he means is that such deeds in particular and deeds of righteousness in general should not be done in such a way that those who practice them get the credit rather than God. The issue at stake is more than just a pure attitude, forgetfulness of self, or conversion of the heart. It means effectively preventing a good deed from recoiling upon the one who does it. The emphasis does not lie upon God as the one for whose sake the deed is done. In the case of almsgiving and fasting, the point that matters is avoiding publicity.[75] Private prayer should be offered in one's own room. It is no accident that the postscript to the Lord's prayer in 6:14–15, the only petition Matthew enlarges upon, is one that involves other human beings. Prayer makes us ready to forgive "men" (cf. 5:44b) if that is not clear to them already.

Matt. 6:1–18 does not simply continue the description of the better righteousness of Jesus' disciples, nor does it provide an interpretation of that righteousness. It is like a series of guidelines to a law. One could hardly expect anything else, if, as we have shown, 5:17–48 forms a single whole. The same holds good for the following sections of the Sermon on the Mount. Hence it does not matter that there are no further headings like the one in 6:1.[76]

In 6:19 we have the beginning of a new series of instructions concerned with wealth and its acquisition. These instructions extend as far as 6:34, and in Matthew's eyes they constitute the next section of the Sermon on the Mount. True, the conclusion is more clearly marked than the beginning, not least by Matthew's favorite catchword, "righteousness" in v. 33 and the closing statement in v. 34. Matthew was probably not responsible for this closing statement, but it was definitely he who inserted it at this point. But the beginning and end of the section correspond to one another in subject matter. Vv. 33–34 say clearly what vv. 19–21 were hinting at when they spoke of laying up treasures on earth which was the wrong thing to do, and laying up treasures in heaven, i.e., merits, which are necessary for those who would seek God's kingdom and his righteousness, without being anxious for the morrow. I interpret the positive injunction as a challenge to realize the righteousness which God demands. It is emphatically "his" righteousness. This recalls 5:16. We are not to think of our own salvation; that is only meant as an indirect incentive to laying up treasure in heaven. The prohibition is concerned with the preservation of life, not with lack of care in other things.

Only the negative side of these themes is developed. Earning money is dangerous because it draws the heart away from God (vv. 19–24). Moreover, it is unnecessary and a sign of little faith, because God cares for his little children (vv. 25–32).[77] At this point, if we lay no particular stress on the word "tomorrow" in v. 34, Matthew seems to permit anxiety, including earning bread for "today." 6:1–18 is hardly meant to encourage mendicancy! The section is attached more closely to the preceding section than it is to the antitheses. The link between the two sections is the strong emphasis on the idea of the reward,[78] although this theme is not developed in a positive direction. If 6:19–34 is concerned with the refusal of pecuniary gain, apart from the day's minimum, the reason is that 6:1–18 takes it for granted that the disciples are living in comfortable though modest circumstances. For such a life it was necessary to lay down guidelines.[79] This means that 6:19–34 expresses in detail what was implied in 5:16. The disciples become the lights of the world only by fulfilling the commandments, not e.g., by success in business.

There remain eleven verses consisting of groups of sayings in 7:1–5 and 7–11. These groups of sayings had already been combined before Matthew. There is also the saying between the two groups, 7:6. It is not immediately obvious what connection there is between the two groups themselves and with the rest of the Sermon on the Mount. Many see no connection at all. Others regard 7:1–11 not as a section, but as a series of loosely connected sayings.[80] Now it is hardly conceivable that Matthew was merely appending a series of miscellaneous items. Why should he have separated 7:1–5 (and it was he who did so) from its traditional connection with 5:48?[81] 7:7–11 would have have fitted in easily after 6:5–15. All the same, vv. 1–5, 6, and 7–11 have this much in common: they make the reaction of other people the criterion to decide whether something should be done or left undone. This applies also to 7:12a. Of course, the golden rule sums it all up by including the law and the prophets in v. 12b and by its allusion to 5:17. This connects it not simply with what immediately precedes, but with the whole body of the Sermon on the Mount. But Matthew's procedure in selecting this formulation and shifting it from its earlier context in connection with the love of enemy (Luke 6:31) is easily explained if the preceding text suggested it. Accordingly, we should try to read vv. 1–11 as an expression of a common theme. This is the respect which we owe to "men." We may ask whether in 7:1–11 Matthew is not thinking about the reaction of those before whom the disciples are supposed to show their good works.[82] If so, 7:1–5 means: Do not pry into their peccadilloes. If you do, they will turn upon you.[83] If that is the correct interpretation, the "brother" of vv. 3–5 can hardly mean the brother in the faith. If it did, we would have to take these verses as a parenthesis: vv. 1–2 apply to the Christian brother even more. V. 6 fits in nicely with our suggested theme. No matter whether it is applied to the non-Christian brother or to apostates, when people threaten you, you have lost nothing so long as they do you no harm. This would be the only qualification to vv. 1–5.[84] Vv. 7–11 do not fit in easily under any interpretation. At first sight, it looks attractive if we read on at vv. 7–8: Ask men for things instead of judging them, and they will accept you. But because of v. 11, the petition mentioned in vv. 7–8 must be addressed to God, and it is he who grants our requests. So we should probably take it like this: Pray to God that men may listen to you and for wisdom to treat them properly, and he will grant your request. It is impossible to be certain, but it is not unlikely that Matthew intended 7:1–11 as a section on a single theme and like the preceding sections to come under the heading of 5:16.

The conclusion of the Sermon on the Mount, 7:13–27,[85] again underscores the judgment motif we have met before. Those who fail to do God's will cannot enter the kingdom. Confession with the lips is not enough. It fits in with what we have discovered thus far that Matthew should exemplify this warning in 17:15–23, not with evil doers as he does in 25:41ff., but with those who invoke the name of Jesus for their prophesyings and miracles, yet from the outside (cf. 5:12; 10:41; 23:34). They have also been guilty of lawlessness in other connections, not in their prophetic and miraculous activity.[86] To its very end, the Sermon on the Mount is concerned with the missionary endeavors of Jesus' disciples.[87] And in the last resort, prophetic and miraculous powers, while not depreciated, are nevertheless subordinated to the fulfillment of the divine will.

6.

Aside from a few refinements, an analysis of the structure of the Sermon on the Mount would therefore look something like this:

I. Introduction: 5:3–16; The certainty of the future for Jesus' disciples and their commission in the world.
   A. Rejoice, you disciples. You are spiritually poor and you hunger for the will of your heavenly Father to be done in heaven as well as on earth. A sure future in heaven awaits you (5:3–12).
   B. But as long as the world endures, you are as necessary for

the world around you as salt and light. Let them see your good works in which you perform your Father's will. Then they will acknowledge you. That is your mission in the world (5:13–16).

II. The body of the Sermon: 5:17–7:12; Instructions to the disciples for their commission in the world.

A. The will of God: 5:17–48

1. I have come to assert the perfect will of my Father as expressed in the law and the prophets against the restrictions placed upon it in Jewish interpretation. Your fulfillment of the commandments must therefore be different from that of the Jews, absolutely different. Otherwise you will not be admitted to the kingdom (5:17–20).

2. Jewish restrictions on the commandments, contrasted with their true sense and illustrated:
The fifth commandment (5:21–26),
The sixth commandment (5:27–30, 31–32),
The prohibition of oaths (5:33–37),
The prohibition of resistance (5:38–42),
The love commandment (5:43–47),

3. Therefore be perfect like your heavenly Father (5:48).

B. Guidelines for fulfillment: 6:1–7:12

1. Do not fulfill the commandments in the way so many Jews do, seeking credit for yourselves rather than for God. Otherwise you will have no reward in the kingdom (6:1).
Illustrations (6:2–18):
Give alms only in secret (6:2–4).
Say your prayers only when no one is watching and keep them short, not like the Gentiles; the Lord's Prayer (6:5–15).
Fast only when no one is watching (6:16–18).

2. First carry out your commission and only then take thought for your own security (6:19–34):
Do not seek financial profit; it draws your heart away from God (6:19–24).
Do not be anxious about food and clothing. Your

Father gives what is necessary to those who have made his will their life's goal; work only for the day's minimum (6:25–34).

3. Pay respect to those to whom you are sent (7:1–11). Don't pry into their sins, otherwise they may turn on you. If they react with open hostility, you have discharged your obligation (7:6).

Pray to your Father for a good reception by others, and he will grant your request (7:7–11).

C. Summary: 7:12

The golden rule summarizes the Father's will as expressed in the law and prophets, insofar as it applies to the disciples' commission in the world.

III. Conclusion: 7:13–27; The disciples warned against failure to fulfill their commission in the world.

A. Pursue the narrow and lonely way which is the way your commission takes you, because it is the way to eternal life. Avoid the broad way where multitudes are rushing headlong into eternal destruction (7:13–14).

B. In particular, keep away from all false prophets. They may prophesy in my name and perform miracles, but they are not carrying out the commission which consists in the fulfillment of my Father's will (7:15–23).

C. Everyone who lives up to his commission is concerned that people should acknowledge the Father's will. Such a one behaves wisely and will stand firm in the day of judgment. He who fails in his commission is behaving foolishly and will not pass the test (7:24–27).

7.

Thus Matthew did not compose the Sermon on the Mount in order to unfold "the gospel of the kingdom" as he believed Jesus proclaimed it in his public ministry. To this extent it is not a sermon. It embodies instructions for the disciples, i.e., for all who on the basis of the gospel have committed themselves to the narrow way of discipleship which leads to the kingdom, and who "observe all that I have commanded you" (Matt. 28:20). But it is not a complete outline of Jesus' ethic. It is only one aspect of it, the aspect of discipleship. And even that aspect is limited to the task of preaching the gospel to those outside the faith. It describes the kind of behavior that will enlist others as disciples. That is why the Sermon ignores other matters, e.g., how to preach the gospel, or the common life of the disciples. All that comes up for treatment later (chaps. 10 and 18). There are no general legislative maxims anywhere in Matthew. As for the broad way which leads to destruction, those who travel on it are left to their own devices.

The theme of the Sermon on the Mount is enunciated at 5:16, right at the end of the introduction (5:3–16). The body of the Sermon (5:17–7:12) carries out that theme. In the first part, which is basic to the whole (5:17–48), Matthew explains what Jesus commanded. It was no new law but the unqualified will of God as it stood and still stands in the Old Testament commandments. Of course, Matthew does not regard the commandments as a collection of detailed instructions coming down straight from God. They simply unfold the ground rules of ethics. Insofar as they relate to discipleship as a commission to spread the gospel, they are summarized in the commandment of love, or alternatively in the golden rule (7:12). Part two lays down guidelines for behavior (6:1–7:11). The conclusion (7:13–27) drives the point home: Anyone who fails to make discipleship, the commission to spread the gospel, his goal, is rushing headlong into eternal destruction. He is like so many Christian prophets and wonderworkers who think their mission is something different from living out the will of God before the world around them.

NOTES

1. Matt. 28:16–20. This pericope represents Matthew's resurrection appearance. Unlike Luke and John he does not make the risen One reveal anything that is really new. Moreover, the opening claim to authority (to preach, to teach, and to heal) is exactly what he had been doing during the earthly ministry. But it is now universalized as the result of the Easter event. On the latter see R. Kratz, *Auferweckung als Befreiung. Eine Studie zur Passions- und Auferstehungstheologie des Matthäus (besonders Mt. 27, 62–28, 15)* (SBS 65; Stuttgart, 1973). This, together with the promise of divine assistance, serves to ratify the teaching of the earthly Jesus and to make discipleship possible. Even the command to baptize, which is sometimes thought to be new, is not entirely so. John had baptized all the Jews (3:5) and Jesus himself had endorsed baptism as a requirement of "righteousness" (see below, note 48) (3:15). While he was pursuing his earthly ministry independently among the Jews (10:5–6) there was no need for any further baptisms. On Matt. 28:16–20 see, e.g., G. Bornkamm, "Der Auferstandene und der Irdische. Mt. 28, 16–20" in E. Dinkler and H. Thyen (eds.), *Zeit und Geschichte* (Bultmann Festschrift; Tübingen, 1964), 171–91, repr. in Bornkamm *et al.*, *Überlieferung und Auslegung im Matthäusevangelium* (WMANT 1; Neukirchen-Vluyn, 1960,[6] 1970), 289–310 (not in ET); and most recently J. Lange, *Das Erscheinen des Auferstandenen im Evangelium nach Matthäus. Eine traditions- und redaktionsgeschichtliche Untersuchung zu Mt. 28, 16–20* (Forschungen zur Bibel 11; Würzburg, 1973).

2. Much of the recent influence of the Sermon on the Mount (for the earlier period see É. Massaux, *L'influence de l'Évangile de Saint Matthieu sur la littérature chrétienne avant Saint Irénée* [Universitas Catholica Lovanensis, Diss. theol. II 42; Louvain, 1950]) is to be found on the periphery or outside the church, where exegesis often runs riot. Histories of interpretation generally seem to confine themselves to the recognized literature. See E. Fascher, "Bergpredigt II. Auslegungsgeschichtlich," RGG[3] 1 (1957) cols. 1050–53 on Marx, Tolstoy, and Kautsky. In English see W. S. Kissinger, *The Sermon on the Mount: A History of In-*

terpretation and Bibliography (ATLABS 2; Metuchen, N.J., 1975). Even today the Sermon on the Mount is cited freely by politicians (e.g., K. Matthiesen, "Wer von Mitleid spricht, wird ausgelacht," *Frankfurter Rundschau,* November 4, 1974), 12. The Sermon on the Mount even figures in court cases, esp. in connection with the draft. "By contrast, it plays a surprisingly minor role in the ecumenical discussion of ethical problems, and the same is true in theological ethics." So L. Goppelt, "Das Problem der Bergpredigt. Jesu Gebot und die Wirklichkeit dieser Welt," in *Christologie und Ethik. Aufsätze zum Neuen Testament* (Göttingen, 1968), 27–43, esp. 27. Is that still true? On recent ecumenical discussion see C. Krause, "Die Bergpredigt in den ökumenischen Studien seit dem zweiten Weltkrieg," *LR* 18 (1968), 65–79.

3. Matthew 5–7; 10; 13; 18 and 24–25 are universally described as "discourses." This is all right for the first two if all that is meant is that they are extended speeches, without regard to their form, function, or occasion. Guidelines for the ministry of a limited circle of disciples would hardly pass for a discourse today. Chap. 13 is a sequence of four scenes where Jesus speaks alternately to the people (vv. 1–9, 24–35) and to the disciples (vv. 10–23, 36–52), and before the last section there is a distinct change of venue. Chap. 18 is a doctrinal disquisition in reply to two questions addressed to Jesus by the disciples. According to E. Schweizer, *Matthäus und seine Gemeinde* (SBS 71; Stuttgart, 1974), 106–7, the complex actually starts at 17:24. Chaps. 24–25 are a private indoctrination of the disciples in reply to a question, though it is interrupted. But in looking at the structure of Matthew 13 we are led to ask whether chap. 23 ought not to be counted as a part of the complex. Cf. W. Trilling, *Das wahre Israel. Studien zur Theologie des Matthäus–Evangeliums* (SANT 10; Munich, 1964), 95. Is that why the story of the widow's mite is omitted?

4. I assume with most scholars that the Sermon on the Mount is based upon a compilation of sayings composed or transmitted by Q. It is featured in Luke 6:20–49 as the Sermon on the Plain, where it is reproduced in a form fairly close to the original in

length and order. Cf. in general M. Devisch, "Le document Q, source de Matthieu. Problématique actuelle" in M. Didier (ed.) *L'Évangile selon Matthieu. Rédaction et théologie* (BETS 29; Gembloux, 1972), 71–97. Only a part of the extra material and the variations come from the later development of Q prior to Matthew. Cf. D. Lührmann, *Die Redaktion der Logienquelle* (WMANT 33; Neukirchen-Vluyn, 1969), 104–21. This was not necessarily a literary process involving written documents of papyrus or parchment, but part of the continued transmission of the Sermon in oral form. Not everything which happened to the discourse material in practice need necessarily have stood written in Matthew's copy of Q. This is the element of truth in the position of those scholars who are skeptical about Q, such as J. Jeremias, *The Sermon on the Mount* (Philadelphia, 1963), who thinks that the Sermon was shaped entirely on oral tradition (he calls it "an early Christian catechism"); or H.-T. Wrege, *Die Überlieferungs- geschichte der Bergpredigt* (WUNT 9; Tübingen, 1968), who persistently and often convincingly shows that Matthew and Luke cannot be derived from one and the same document. This does not answer the question as to whether any given fragment of Matthew is a community formation or an editorial composition. So emphatically H. Frankemölle, "Die Makarismen (Mt 5, 1–12; Lk 6, 20–23). Motive und Umfang der redaktionellen Komposition," *BZ* n.s. 15 (1971), 52–75. Cf. further C. H. Lohr, "Oral Techniques in the Gospel of Matthew," *CBQ* 23 (1961), 403–35.

5. F. Hahn, "Methodologische Überlegungen zur Rückfrage nach Jesus," in K. Kertelge (ed.), *Rückfrage nach Jesus. Zur Methodik und Bedeutung der Frage nach dem historischen Jesus* (Quaestiones disputatae 63; Freiburg/Basel/Wien, 1974), 11–77. D. Lührmann, "Liebet eure Feinde (LK 6, 27–36/Mt 5, 39–48)" *ZTK* 69 (1972), 412–438. D. Lührmann, "Die Frage nach Kriterien für ursprüngliche Jesusworte. Eine Problemskizze" in J. Dupont (ed.), *Jésus aux origines de la christologie* (BETL 40; Gembloux, 1975). It is too late now for conservatives to argue for the authenticity of the Sermon on the Mount. Yet it is premature to abandon the quest of the historical Jesus in this connection as proposed by L. Schottroff, "Der Mensch Jesus im Spannungsfeld

von Politischer Theologie und Aufklärung," *TP* 8 (1973), 243–57. So long as the discussion is in its present stage it would be wiser to avoid speaking of Jesus when what we mean is the literary figure or the shape of the tradition. To this extent we cannot call the Sermon on the Mount a "collection of the sayings of Jesus."

6. See, however, J. Kürzinger, "Zur Komposition der Bergpredigt nach Matthäus," *Bibl.* 40 (1969), 569–89; J. Dupont, *Les Béatitudes* (3 vols.; Paris, 1957–1973); G. Eichholz, "Die Aufgabe einer Auslegung der Bergpredigt," in *Tradition und Interpretation. Studien zum Neuen Testament und zur Hermeneutik* (ThB 29; Munich, 1965), 35–56; U. Luck, *Die Vollkommenheitsforderung der Bergpredigt. Ein aktuelles Kapitel der Theologie des Matthäus* (ThEx 150; Munich, 1968); O. Hanssen, "Zum Verständnis der Bergpredigt. Eine missionstheologische Studie zu Mt. 5, 17–18," in E. Lohse (ed.), *Der Ruf Jesu und die Antwort der Gemeinde* (Jeremias Festschrift; Göttingen, 1970), 94–111; M. Hengel, "Leben in der Veränderung. Ein Beitrag zum Verständnis der Bergpredigt," *EvKomm* 3 (1970), 647–51; M. D. Goulder, *Midrash and Lection in Matthew* (London, 1974), 250–69, etc.; also W. D. Davies, *The Setting of the Sermon on the Mount* (Cambridge, 1969), who, however, does not deal with the text itself but with "the circumstances of its emergence and formulation" (abbreviated in *The Sermon on the Mount* [London, 1966]). Not accessible to me was P. Pokorný, *Der Kern der Bergpredigt. Eine Auslegung* (Hamburg, 1969). A history of recent interpretation of Matthew as a whole will be found in Didier (ed.), *L'Evangile*. See also W. G. Kümmel, *Introduction to the New Testament* (New York/Nashville, 1975), 101–21; A. Sand, *Das Gesetz und die Propheten. Untersuchungen zur Theologie des Evangeliums nach Matthäus* (BU 11; Regensburg, 1974), 1–31.

7. Whether on its own or in conjunction with 4:12ff. is unimportant here.

8. That 9:35 is meant to recall 4:23 is shown by v. 36, where Jesus sees the masses directly. This is not just an awkward editing of Mark 6:34. Matthew expects his readers or his audience to keep in mind the effect Jesus had on the crowds as stated in 4:24–

25. That chaps. 5–9 form a continuous section is a commonly held opinion. Goulder differs; as we have seen, he argues that Matthew was designed to be a lectionary. The sequence of discourse followed by miracles is implicit in Mark 1 and explicit in Q. It would be worthwhile extending our structural analysis beyond the shorter and longer sections of the Sermon, but I do not wish to get involved in the analysis of the gospel as a whole. The most recent treatment of this subject will be found in Schweizer, *Matthäus und seine Gemeinde*, 15–31. On Matt. 28:16–20 see note 1, and section 4.

9. J. Schniewind, *Das Evangelium nach Matthäus* (NTD 2; Göttingen, 1937; [12]1968), 37–106; P. Hoffmann, "Die Stellung der Bergpredigt im Matthäusevangelium. Auslegung der Bergpredigt I," *BibLeb* (1969), 57–65, esp. 62. Further advocates of the christological interpretation are listed in C. Burger, "Jesu Taten nach Matthäus 8 und 9," *ZThK* 70 (1973), 272–87, esp. 272–73. Burger himself argues for an ecclesiological rather than christological interpretation of chaps. 8–9. On the composition of these chapters see further H. Held, "Matthew as Interpreter of the Miracle Stories," in G. Bornkamm *et al., Tradition and Interpretation in Matthew* (Philadelphia, 1963), 165–299, esp. 246ff.; W. G. Thompson, "Reflections on the Composition of Matthew 8:1–9:34," *CBQ* 33 (1971), 365–88.

10. So e.g., Schniewind, 36–37; cautiously E. Schweizer, *The Good News According to Matthew* (Atlanta, 1975), 76–78; Burger, 282, offers a curious interpretation, taking the proclamation and healings merely as a reference to, not as a list of the contents of chaps. 8–9.

11. G. Strecker, *Der Weg der Gerechtigkeit. Untersuchung zur Theologie des Matthäus* (FRLANT 82; Göttingen, 1963 = [3]1971), 126–28.

12. Strecker, *Weg*, 128–30; P. Stuhlmacher, *Das paulinische Evangelium I. Vorgeschichte* (FRLANT 95; Göttingen, 1968), 238–43. On the kingdom see A. Kretzer, *Die Herrschaft der Himmel und die Söhne des Reiches. Eine redaktionsgeschichtliche Untersuchung zum Basileiabegriff und Basileiaverständnis im Matthäusevangelium* (SBM 10; Würzburg/Stuttgart, 1971).

13. Strecker, *Weg,* 106–07, 116; S. van Tilborg, *The Jewish Leaders in Matthew* (Leiden, 1972), 142–65.

14. One may hesitate whether to translate it "the" or "a" mountain. "Mountain range," (so Schniewind, 39; cf. W. Grundmann, *Das Evangelium nach Matthäus* [ThHK 1; Berlin, 1968, ²1971], 114) is ruled out by the context, where there is no suggestion of a journey. On the mountain theme in Matthew see Strecker, *Weg,* 98; Lange, 392–446. In view of what follows, Sinai or Moses typology seems to me improbable. Cf. Lange, 440–45.

15. Strecker, *Weg,* 191–206; R. Schnackenburg, "Ihr seid das Salz der Erde, das Licht der Welt. Zu Mt. 5, 13–16," in *Mélanges E. Cardinal Tisserant* (StT 231; Vatican City, 1964) I, 365–87; U. Luz, "Die Jünger im Matthäusevangelium," *ZNW* 62 (1971), 141–71; van Tilborg, 99–141; Lange, 308–26.

16. Jeremias, *Sermon,* 26, "like a red thread." In Matthew God is the Father of mankind in general. It is another question whether the Sermon is addressed wholly or in part to a particular group of disciples (see Section 4).

17. Luck, 14–15; H. Conzelmann, *Outline of the Theology of the New Testament* (London, 1968), 123.

18. So M. Dibelius, *The Sermon on the Mount* (New York: 1940), esp. 16; Goppelt, *Aufsätze,* 41, and many others. Grundmann, *Matthäus,* 111, and U. Wilckens, *Das Neue Testament* (Hamburg/Cologne/Zurich, 1970, ³1971), 25–26, draw the logical conclusion that 4:23–5:1 constitutes a single pericope.

19. There is no comprehensive study of Matthean style. J. Jeremias has both orally and in writing called repeated attention to the material in A. Schlatter, *Der Evangelist Matthäus. Seine Sprache, sein Ziel, seine Selbstständigkeit* (Stuttgart, 1929, ⁶1963). With Luke we have on the whole come much further.

20. Hanssen's stimulating investigation has been insufficiently noticed (see below, note 76). Sand, *Gesetz,* 46 is skeptical about it: "no 'discourse,' with only a single theme carried to its logical conclusion."

21. A. Huck-H. Lietzmann-F. L. Cross, *A Synopsis of the First Three Gospels* (Tübingen, 1936) provides the Sermon on the Mount with subtitles indicating the content. Matt. 7:24–27 is

entitled "Schlussgleichnisse," (closing parables) which, however, is a functional and formal description. It is certainly correct to describe this material as parabolic so far as the earlier stages of the tradition are concerned, but it is really a double parable. Matthew probably regards it as an allegory (see below, note 87). The titles are often too vague. "Righteousness before God," (so Schweizer, *Matthew,* 136) does not sufficiently distinguish 6:1–18 from 5:21–48, which he entitles "The New Righteousness," (110). As so often, Schweizer's subtitles do not correspond to the text.

22. Most recently e.g., Dupont, *Béatitudes;* N. Walter, "Die Bearbeitung der Seligpreisungen durch Matthäus" in F. L. Cross (ed.), *Studia Evangelica* (TU 102; Berlin, 1968) 4:246–58; P. Hoffmann, " 'Selig sind die Armen . . .' Auslegung der Bergpredigt II (Mt. 5, 3–16)," *BibLeb* 10 (1969), 111–22; G. Strecker, "Die Makarismen der Bergpredigt," *NTS* 17 (1970/71), 255–75. On the form, a series with a lengthy concluding item, see also D. Daube, *The New Testament and Rabbinic Judaism* (London, 1956), 196–201.

23. So emphatically Strecker, "Makarismen."

24. Frankemölle, "Makarismen," 72–73. Unlike him, Dupont, Walter, and others, I assume with Strecker, "Makarismen," and Lührmann, "Liebet," 415, that vv. 7–9, and perhaps even v. 5 are pre-Matthean. Vv. 3/10b constitute a typically Matthean inclusio (cf. 5:17/7:12; 6:25/34a).

25. So Strecker, "Makarismen." I find it difficult, at least in vv. 3 and 8.

26. On this see most recently D. R. A. Hare, *The Theme of Jewish Persecution of Christians in the Gospel According St. Matthew* (SNTSMS 6; Cambridge, 1967).

27. On Matthean ecclesiology see e.g., Strecker, *Weg,* 191–242, 253–56, and most recently H. Frankemölle "Jahwebund und Kirche Christi. Studien zur Form- und Traditionsgeschichte des 'Evangeliums' nach Matthäus," *NTA* n.s. 10 (Münster, 1973); Schweizer, *Gemeinde.*

28. If Lührmann, "Makarismen," is right, Matthew may have covered up the traditional connections between the beatitudes and the section on love for the enemy. *Contra* Goulder, who, follow-

ing A. M. Farrer, *St Matthew and St Mark* (London, 1954, ²1966), regards the whole Sermon as an exposition of the beatitudes. Against Farrer, see Davies, *Setting,* 9–12.

29. In the sense of sincere discipleship, not of perfection already attained. Matthew is aware that Christians can still sin.

30. See e.g., H. Windisch, *The Meaning of the Sermon on the Mount. A Contribution to the Historical Understanding of the Gospels and to the Problem of Their True Exegesis* (Philadelphia: Westminster, 1941), 68, note 10.

31. It would be appropriate here to investigate the relationship between the imperative and the indicative. This is an important consideration for the Sermon as a whole, but we have neither the time nor the space to do that here. The motif of reward is also relevant. See most recently Sand, *Gesetz,* 115–20.

32. On the text see among recent works, Schnackenburg; G. Schneider, "Das Bildwort von der Lampe. Zur Traditionsgeschichte eines Jesus-Wortes," *ZNW* 61 (1970), 183–209, esp. 199–202; F. Hahn, "Die Worte vom Licht Lk. 11, 33–36," in P. Hoffmann *et al.* (eds.) *Orientierung an Jesus. Zur Theologie der Synoptiker* (J. Schmid Festschrift; Freiburg/Basel/Wien, 1973), 107–38, esp. 117–119.

33. This is either an allegorical reference to the last judgment or, if "by men" is taken literally (cf. v. 16), it means "then you will deserve persecution, and you will not enjoy the protection promised" in 28:20. For the formulation cf. *Joseph and Aseneth* 13:11. Does this imply an urban situation?

34. Like vv. 13a and 14a, v. 16 will be Matthean. So most recently Schneider, 200–01.

35. Apart from the commentaries *ad loc* see D. Lührmann, *Das Offenbarungsverständnis bei Paulus und in paulinischen Gemeinden* (WMANT 16; Neukirchen-Vluyn, 1965), 49–54; W. C. van Unnik, "Die Rücksicht auf die Reaktion der Nicht-Christen als Motiv in der altchristlichen Paränese," in W. Eltester (ed.) *Judentum Urchristentum Kirche* (J. Jeremias Festschrift; BZNW 26; Berlin, 1960, ²1964), 221–34.

36. On the text see most recently E. Käsemann, *An die Römer* (HNT 8a; Tübingen, 1973, ³1974) *ad loc.* (ET forthcoming).

Whether this is a specific reference to the scholars may be left open. Even such a person would be treated simply as a typical Jew.

37. Parallel notions, more relevant for the Matthean tradition, are instanced in E. Schweizer, "Der Jude im Verborgenen . . . , dessen Lob nicht von Menschen sondern von Gott kommt. Zu Röm. 2,28f und Mt. 6,1–18," in J. Gnilka (ed.), *Neues Testament und Kirche* (R. Schnackenburg Festschrift; Freiburg/Basel/Wien, 1974), 115–24, repr. in E. Schweizer, *Gemeinde,* 86–97. We are not claiming that Matthew stands within the Pauline tradition, but rather that both of them stand in the same tradition—emanating perhaps from Antioch? On the historical aspect of the connection between Paul and Matthew, which is hardly to be separated from the systematic aspect, see the recent discussions by Davies, *Setting,* 316–41; A. Sand, "Die Polemik gegen die 'Gesetzlosigkeit' im Evangelium nach Matthäus und bei Paulus," *BZ* n.s. 14 (1970), 112–25; Goulder, *Midrash,* 153–70 who thinks Matthew knew all the Pauline epistles.

38. Deeds of charity are distinguished from the detailed injunctions of the Torah. Nevertheless they are regarded as obligatory. They may be subdivided into gifts and works of love. See Billerbeck IV: 536–610; J. Jeremias, "Die Salbungsgeschichte Mc. 14, 3–9," *ZNW* 35 (1936), 75–82, repr. in *Abba,* 107–15. Many interpret these injunctions in this sense or still more narrowly as works of charity. But they are not necessarily good works in the sense of 1 Pet. 2:12, the Pastoral Epistles, or Philo.

39. Schnackenburg, arguing against the predominant view in recent interpretation, makes only Schweizer (178) an exception.

40. This suggestion goes back to Schlatter, *Matthäus,* 146, and it is strongly advocated by Hanssen. How precisely baptism and teaching interpret the idea of allowing the light of good works to shine forth and vice versa is something that requires explanation. 5:16, in my opinion, does not refer primarily to preaching. Conversely, the Sermon on the Mount is not to be identified in an unqualified sense with "all that I have commanded you." It is only a part of that. As I see it, 28:16–20 is not thinking of mission in the sense of the charge to "go into all the world" (the participle "going" is only an expletive as often in Matthew) nor is 5:16.

41. Cf. G. Eichholz, *Auslegung der Bergpredigt* (BS 46; Neukirchen-Vluyn, 1965), 59–60, who, however, points to Luke 5:1–11. In that case "service of the word" is precisely *not* the meaning of "catching men" despite Schniewind, *Matthäus,* 35.

42. For the text see H. Hübner, *Das Gesetz in der synoptischen Tradition. Studien zur These einer progressiven Qumranisierung und Judaisierung innerhalb der synoptischen Tradition* (Witten, 1973) 15–39, etc.; E. Schweizer, "Noch einmal Mt. 5, 17–20" in H. Balz, and S. Schulz (eds.), *Das Wort und die Wörter* (G. Friedrich Festschrift; Stuttgart/Cologne/Mainz, 1973), 69–73, repr. in Schweizer, *Gemeinde,* 78–85.

43. On the form and its origin see Lührmann, *Redaktion,* 116–18. That does not rule out the possibility that it was Matthew who shaped vv. 17 (cf. 10:34) and 20, or at least considerably reshaped them.

44. In v. 17 the word "or" fits only the action of relaxing. The prophets (which interpreters frequently ignore here: Sand, *Gesetz,* 197–205) are certainly distinguished from the law, but they are hardly a second source of legislation. Rather, they are protectors and expositors of the law (cf. Hos. 6:6 cited at Matt. 9:13 and 12:7). For "fulfill" in the above sense see Matt. 3:15. The introductions to the fulfillment quotations are no less Matthean than 5:17. See Strecker, *Weg,* 50; W. Rothfuchs, *Die Erfüllungszitate des Matthäus-Evangeliums. Eine biblisch-theologische Untersuchung* (BWANT 88; Stuttgart/Berlin/Cologne/Mainz, 1969), 44–56. But their passive form, in contrast to the active form in 3:15 and 5:17, is not unimportant from a semantic point of view. See further below, note 46. On "to do and to teach" see TestLev 13,3.

45. On this distinction see C. Burchard, "Das doppelte Liebesgebot in der frühen christlichen Überlieferung," in Lohse (ed.), *Ruf Jesu,* 39–63, esp. 53–54. "Of these" refers back to vv. 17–18, though to which precise point is irrelevant. Perhaps it was originally a superfluous demonstrative (so Wrege, 41, note 3). But it no longer serves that purpose in Matthew.

46. In 5:17 "I have come," as in 10:34, is not intended in an exclusive sense. There is therefore nothing to rule out the claim that in Matthew's redactional Christology the prophecies are "fulfilled"

in Jesus. Thus we may hold both explanations together. All I ask is whether both concerns are expressed in 5:17–20, as Schweizer, *Matthew,* contends. The relation between doing and teaching is a subject for further exploration in connection with Matthew's Christology as well as with his ecclesiology.

47. On the difficult phrase "until all comes to pass" see most recently Schweizer, "Noch einmal," who says it refers to the law, not to apocalyptic events. In the present context it prepares the way for v. 19. What applies to life in the kingdom is not within the present purview, nor as I see it, anywhere else in the Sermon on the Mount. So we should be careful not to talk about "justice in the reign of God," as does Luck, 21, or "royal law of the kingdom," as he and others do. What it means is the good, old law.

48. On "righteousness" in Matthew see e.g., Strecker, *Weg,* 149–58; Sand, *Gesetz,* 197–205. The passages cited are all insertions of the evangelist (3:15; 5:6, 10, 21; 6:1, 33; 21:32).

49. Thus many, e.g., G. Barth, "Matthew's Understanding of the Law" in Bornkamm, Barth, and Held, *Tradition,* 58–164, esp. 75, 159–64. See e.g., the critique by Strecker in *Weg,* 137, note 4; Sand, 99–104.

50. The contrast here is different from that in 23:2–3, although no contradiction is involved. Cf., 23:23.

51. On the text see H. Braun, *Spätjüdisch-häretischer und frühchristlicher Radikalismus. Jesus von Nazareth und die essenische Qumransekte* (BHTh 24; Tübingen, 1957, ²1969) esp. II *passim;* Conzelmann, *Outline,* 120–24; M. J. Suggs, *Wisdom, Christology, and Law in Matthew's Gospel* (Cambridge, Mass., 1970), 109–15; *idem* "The Antitheses as Redactional Products," below, pp. 93ff.; Lührmann, "Liebet"; Hübner, *Gesetz,* 40–112, 230–36, etc.; Sand, *Gesetz,* 46–56. It is misleading that the term "antithesis" is sometimes used for both the thesis and the antithesis together, sometimes only for the second part, and sometimes for the antithetical form itself.

52. Goppelt, *Christologie,* is an exception (note 64).

53. Does Matthew think of Moses as the author (cf. 19:8), or does he use the passive formula to suggest that the theses are anonymous?

54. G. Barth, *Tradition,* 93–94; R. Hummel, *Die Auseinandersetzung zwischen Kirche und Judentum im Matthäusevangelium* (BEvTh 33; Munich; 1963, ²1966), 71–72; cf. Sand, *Gesetz,* 48.

55. Often in the context of the distinction between "genuine" (i.e., where the antithesis is strictly related to the thesis, not in the sense of an authentic Jesus saying) and improper, or primary and secondary in a literary sense (i.e., when parallels to the antithesis occur in Luke). Thus we get two groups, the first, second, and fourth, and the third, fifth, and sixth, on which judgment is often passed *en bloc.* For objections against the use of criteria to distinguish between the various antitheses with regard to their authenticity see J. Jeremias, *New Testament Theology I. The Proclamation of Jesus* (New York, 1971), who argues that the antithetical form is original to all the antitheses; Lührmann, "Liebet," 413.

56. It is equally wrong to say that they serve to bring out the true, pure will of God from the obscurity of the original wording (Dibelius, 93, etc.). That the "cause of murder" is to be overcome along with the anger (Luck, 21) is not stated in the text.

57. E. Lohse, "Ich aber sage euch," in Lohse (ed.), *Ruf Jesu,* 189–203, esp. 196–97.

58. The reasons are given in 11:25–30 and 28:16–20. See above, note 1. On this passage see Suggs, *Wisdom,* 77–83; F. Christ, *Jesus-Sophia. Die Sophia-Christologie bei den Synoptikern* (AThANT 57; Zurich, 1970) 81–119.

59. This supports the view that the first two antitheses at least took shape at the same time, aside from later accretions.

60. Or is it comparable to Matt. 19:4–5 (which should be read as a single sentence, making "and said" part of the quotation, thus combining Gen. 1:27 and 2:24)?

61. Cf. Eichholz, *Auslegung,* 69.

62. This is often interpreted to mean the renunciation of one's rights and the ways and means to get them. Cf. Hübner, *Gesetz,* 85, note 206. From a philological point of view this is hardly the most obvious explanation, nor does it fit the following cases. The meaning is: refraining from putting up resistance to a concrete act of injustice when you are the victim. When you are involved in a lawsuit, you must certainly renounce your rights. When some-

one boxes your ears, don't retaliate in self-defense. When you are coerced, don't put up a fight and don't run away. This interpretation is clearly influenced by the fact that the thesis is taken as a general legal principle. But is there really any evidence to support such an interpretation?

63. Cf. Goppelt, *Christologie,* 30–31.

64. So Goppelt, *Christologie,* 30–33. But his interpretation (cf. also Hanssen, 109–10) from the perspective of the commandment of Jesus founders in the light of Matt. 19:17–21. There the decalogue and the commandment of love are cited as the direct and immediate will of God, as Goppelt himself notes. Moreover, like many others, he assumes that the thesis of the first, second, and fourth antitheses comes from Jesus himself. From what has been said above it will be clear that the evangelist was responsible for all of the theses. See also Suggs, *Wisdom,* 109–15.

65. 5:21b is perhaps taken from 5:22. 5:31 may well come from the pericope on divorce (cf. Matt. 19:7–9). 5:33 is somewhat reminiscent of the opinion expressed by Philo, *De Spec. Leg.* II, 2–38 (the truly virtuous man always refrains from swearing; his word is as good as his bond). 5:43 is phrased as the opposite of 5:44 under the influence of a passage like Tacitus, *Hist.* V 5, which is not exactly friendly toward the Jews. Any connection with Qumran can hardly be substantiated. See Hübner, *Gesetz,* 97–107.

66. Cf. also 9:13; 12:7; 19:18–19. "If you would be perfect" in v. 21, which as everyone knows was to have a long history, can in Matthew's intention hardly mean anything extra. Nor in the light of our interpretation of the antitheses does it contain those features in which Jesus goes beyond the OT. Rather, it corrects v. 20, "all these I have observed." But he has not done so perfectly. Is that why Matthew omits "from my youth" (Mark 10:20)?

67. So now Goulder, 3–27, who also takes it in a biographical sense.

68. Windisch; Luck; Suggs, *Wisdom.*

69. See section 4. The ethos behind the last two antitheses lies closer to the ideal of the "pious man" in *Joseph and Aseneth* whose one major proposition, "not to pay back evil for evil" (*JA* 23:9,

28:5, 10, 14; 29:3) is parallel to Matthew's "resist not evil," and in practice comes very close to the love of one's enemy. Cf. C. Burchard, "Fussnoten zum neutestamentlichen Griechisch," *ZNW* 61 (1970), 157–71, esp. 158–59. I have not yet had access to A. Nissen, *Gott und der Nächste im antiken Judentum. Untersuchungen zum Doppelgebot der Liebe* (WUNT 15; Tübingen, 1974).

70. Contested by Walker. More cautiously Sand, *Gesetz,* 76–105: "only indirectly concerned" with opponents (104).

71. Matthew is not "the Christian answer to Jamnia" as Davies, *Setting,* 315 would have it, at least not in the way he takes it to be.

72. Following E. Klostermann, *Das Matthäusevangelium* (HNT 4; Tübingen, ²1927, ⁴1971), 40; Eichholz, 9–10, 61 and others, against the usual view. This appears in different forms and connects only v. 20 with the antitheses, though it gives 5:17ff. a much wider reference. Jeremias, *Sermon,* 22–23, argues that only 5:20 is the theme of the baptismal catechism represented by the Sermon on the Mount (see above, note 4). This provides a division into three parts: the false righteousness of the scribes (5:21–48) and Pharisees (6:1–18) and the new righteousness of Jesus' disciples (6:19–7:27). As far as Matthew's own intention is concerned, this is ruled out because he does not separate the scribes and Pharisees. See e.g., R. Walker, *Die Heilsgeschichte im ersten Evangelium* (FRLANT 91; Göttingen, 1967), 18; Sand, *Gesetz,* 76–84.

73. When he speaks of hypocrites in 6:1–18, Matthew certainly includes them but he does not mean them primarily or exclusively, otherwise he would have made his point more clearly. See van Tilborg, 8–26.

74. On this point see van Tilborg again, 8–13; B. Gerhardsson, "Geistiger Opferdienst nach Matth. 6, 1–6. 16–21" in H. Baltensweiler and B. Reicke (eds.), *Neues Testament und Geschichte* (O. Cullmann Festschrift; Zürich, 1972), 69–77; Schweizer, "Der Jude"; H.-D. Betz, "Analyse von Mt. 6:1–18," in G. Strecker, *Jesus Christus in Historie und Theologie* (H. Conzelmann Festschrift; Tübingen, 1975), 445–57. On the form see also D. Lührmann, *Redaktion,* 118–19.

75. Thus when he speaks of "anointing" and "washing" in 6:17 Matthew is not underscoring fasting in any positive way, but simply inculcating normal behavior. The verbs signify the omission of the opposite.

76. This point does not come out when the Sermon on the Mount is regarded as the treatment of an ethical theme with subsections. For Hanssen the double commandment of love functions as the theme of the Sermon on the Mount (that there is some justification for making this a title for the antitheses see above, section 5).

  I. 5:21–6:18.   The Christian Community and Judaism.
    A. 5:21–48.   The new relationship to the neighbor.
    B. 6:1–18.   The new relationship to God.
 II. 6:19–7:12.   The Christian Community and the Gentiles.
    A. 6:19–34.   The new relationship to God.
    B. 7:1–12.   The new relationship to the neighbor.

But quite apart from that should not 6:19 be more strongly emphasized if it marks the beginning of a new major section of the body of the Sermon (cf. above, note 20)? And if the Gentiles of 6:32 provide the title, what happens to the mention of them in 6:7?

77. On vv. 19–24 see Hahn, "Worte vom Licht," 124–27. Vv. 25ff. form a little diatribe, a rare phenomenon in the synoptic tradition. The contacts with popular philosophy, which have long been noted, deserve more thoughtful investigation.

78. Cf. Schweizer, *Matthew,* 161.

79. According to Grundmann, *Matthäus,* 206, 217, the main point behind 6:19–34 is to explain the fourth petition of the Lord's Prayer. He finds in the Lord's Prayer the basic clue to the structure of the Sermon on the Mount (204–6). I am not convinced by that suggestion, at least not in the form in which he proposes it. On 7:1–6 see below, note 80. But the suggestion that Matthew has constructed links between the Lord's Prayer and other parts of the Sermon or has noticed links already there (cf. 6:32 with 6:8) is worth considering. Similarly Davies' tripartite division, which he took from *Aboth* 1,2: 1. 5:17–48–The Torah of Jesus; 2. 6:1–18–The True Worship of God; 3. 6:19–7:12–True Obedience (304–15), breaks down at 6:19ff., if not before.

80. Grundmann, *Matthäus,* 217–27 separates 7:1–6, which he regards as an exposition of the fifth petition of the Lord's Prayer, and 7:7–11, which he regards as a concluding confirmation of the whole Sermon.

81. Especially since 5:48 must originally have served as an introduction to 7:1ff. (cf. Luke 6:36–37).

82. Similarly Hanssen, *Gesetz,* 102–3.

83. Cf. Rom. 2:1. There is no reason why Matthew should have understood the passive in 7:1–2 as a reverential periphrasis. But the case is quite different in v. 7.

84. Goulder, 265–66, takes it in quite a different way: "Don't expose what is precious, your brother's character, to the malice of the godless," (265).

85. The location and content correspond to a stylistic law in early Christian parenesis. See G. Bornkamm, "Bergpredigt I. Biblisch," *RGG*[3] cols. 1047–50, esp. 1047. This is the way it is constructed: Basic proposition in positive and negative terms (take the narrow way, not the broad one, vv. 13–14); concretization of the negative part: the "false prophets," who held that they were commissioned in the name of Jesus to prophesy and work miracles, one of many examples of the broad way to destruction, vv. 15–23; —positive and negative generalization: build upon the rock, not upon the sand, vv. 24–27.

86. The parallel in Luke 13:26–27 is also different.

87. Was Matthew thinking in 7:24–27 not so much of behavior in private life as of the building up of the Christian community? Cf. 1 Cor. 3:10ff.

M. JACK SUGGS

The Antitheses
as Redactional Products

An earlier study expressed the opinion that the antitheses of Matthew 5 were all formulated by the evangelist.[1] On reflection, the reasons advanced in support of that judgment appear too facile to carry the weight put on them. And, since the opinion contradicts a long-standing consensus, a reassessment of the evidence is in order.

The assignment of the antitheses to Matthew was initially related to a special view of the nature of the authority to whom the evangelist appeals in the Sermon on the Mount. Since that view has not been substantially altered in the interim and continues to inform my understanding, it should be stated briefly. An important aspect of Matthew's Christology was his identification of Jesus and Sophia. In making that identification, the evangelist stood in the stream of Jewish speculation which asserted: "Wisdom appeared upon earth and lived among men. She is the book of the commandments of God, and the law that endures forever" (Bar. 3:37–4:1). On this basis Matthew was able to incorporate into his own attitude toward the Torah elements which we see as being in conflict with each other. He preserved traditions which were stringently narrow in conserving the "jot and tittle" of the law (5:18); he had a penchant for inserting forms of legal debate[2] into inherited stories (12:5–6; 19:7–8); the antitheses are patently intolerant of scholastic discussion. If we experience these elements as inconsistent, it was not so for Matthew. For him, they were arbitrarily

93

synthesized by appeal to the authority of Jesus as Wisdom-Torah. In principle, there could be no contradiction between the letter of the law and a ruling of Jesus, the embodiment of Torah.[3]

The surfacing of this position (which may be only idiosyncratic[4]), is intended to inform the reader of a perspective which is present behind the paper. The specific position is not essential to the main argument pursued below, although the assumption is made throughout that *for Matthew* the voice heard in the Sermon spoke with an authority which the voice of the historical Jesus would not have possessed for his hearers. That assumption rests on the rudimentary fact that, however faithfully the words of Jesus were preserved and transmitted, the Gospels always deliver them to us as truth guaranteed by the exalted figure of the church's faith, not as sayings of a Galilean teacher commended only by his presence and their inherent power.

If it should develop that Matthew created the antitheses, the use of Matt. 5:21–48 to delineate Jesus' relation to the Torah would require considerable caution. New Testament exegetes have tended to write as if "You have heard . . . but I say" is a compass in terms of which other indications of Jesus' attitude toward the law can be quickly oriented: "Jesus demands radical obedience far transcending mere observance of the letter of the law. The Sermon on the Mount contains a whole series of sayings formulated according to a single pattern: 'You have heard that it was said to the men of old, . . . but I say to you: . . . ' (Matt. 5:21ff.). The law says, 'You shall not kill'; but Jesus declares that even an angry word or animosity is a transgression of this commandment."[5]

The surface implication is that the antithetical formulation goes back to Jesus and provides the essential clue to his attitude toward the law. It is a statement that might have been written by most exegetes, though it would not mean the same thing to all. Some mean quite literally that at least some of the antitheses are genuine sayings of Jesus.[6] More often, probably, the intention is to affirm that, even if the antitheses are not demonstrably genuine, they "formulate aptly" what Jesus might have said.[7] The difficulty is that "You have heard . . . but I say" has the ring of a slogan;

as such, it is fully appropriate to Matthew's programmatic campaign against the Pharisees, but may serve a bias which is inappropriate to Jesus' own situation.

However, whether the form should be assigned to Matthew is precisely the question. And it is a question already answered in the negative by a long-standing consensus which assigns three of the antitheses to a pre-Matthean stage. In current discussion, the generally accepted opinion is frequently advanced with no argument beyond reference to Bultmann's classic statement of the case.[8] Bultmann regarded the examples of the form in Matt. 5:31–32a, 38–39a, 43–44a as secondary formations patterned on the antitheses in 5:21–22, 27–28, 33–37. He adduced four reasons for characterizing the formulations beginning in vv. 21, 27, and 33 as primary. Three of the reasons do not appear to me to be substantive and have, in fact, receded in subsequent discussion. Bultmann's argument that in the "primary" formulations the "prohibition is not abolished, but surpassed" cannot be satisfying in view of the absence of agreement as to which (if any) of the antitheses do indeed abrogate a commandment. The observation that these instances lack the mashal form is a generalization which glosses over the formal problems offered by all six antitheses. That "in distinction to the three secondary formations, these three passages are alike in putting the thesis in the form of a prohibition" is accurate, but it fails to take account of other stylistic considerations which impair the force of the point (e.g., the similar structure of the theses at vv. 33 and 43; nonbiblical expansions of both "primary" and "secondary" theses).

But these points were all subsidiary to Bultmann's basic argument for the primacy of the antitheses in vv. 21, 27, and 33. The essential matter was that "in these passages the antithesis was plainly never an isolated saying, for it is only intelligible in relation to the thesis." Paul Hoffmann has advanced this argument again in an essay which recognizes that only by careful buttressing can it bear the load so long placed on it: "In contrast to these so-called secondary antitheses the first, second, and fourth antitheses are primary. . . . In contrast to the antitheses first mentioned the antithetical form is constitutive for the second group.

Thesis and antithesis are so related to one another that the sayings are intelligible only in relation to one another. These primary antitheses . . . were most probably the model on which the rest of the antitheses were built."[9]

In what sense are the sayings in the supposed primary antitheses unintelligible apart from the theses? The three-membered saying in v. 22 is quite capable of standing independently. The dismemberment to which the verse is frequently subjected (because of its stylistic variance from other antitheses and because of the presumed progression of threats in the series) is encouraged only by the assumption that vv. 21–22a belong together. If "but I say to you" is omitted, v. 22 would—with little alteration—fit comfortably in a context like Matthew 18.[10] Further, the problematic sanction attached to the prohibition of murder in v. 21 is most easily explained if v. 22 was an independent saying from which the sanction was borrowed when the antithesis was created.[11]

The alleged unintelligibility of Matt. 5:34 apart from the accompanying thesis in v. 33 is particularly difficult to understand. The prohibition against swearing exists and is transparently meaningful in the non-antithetical instruction at Jas. 5:12,[12] as everyone knows. The likelihood that v. 34 is of Matthean origin is enhanced by a further consideration. In a discussion of editorial expansions required to fit sayings into new contexts, Bultmann had this to say of a "secondary" formulation: "In the same way we may regard 'But I say to you, Do not resist one who is evil' (Matt. 5:39) as an introduction by Matthew to insert the following saying into the context of interpreting the law." Then, without break, he addresses the "primary" formulation under consideration: "Correspondingly, 'But I say to you, Do not swear at all,' in Matt. 5:34 may very well be a formulation by Matthew in place of an originally simpler form such as 'Swear not!' unless indeed Matthew has himself formulated the whole section vv. 34–37 on the basis of some copy, to which Matt. 23:16–22 may correspond."[13]

Precisely! But such a postulated "simpler form" requires no "You have heard . . . but I say." It needs, not a literary context which includes a thesis, but a cultural context in which the customary use (or abuse) of oaths makes the prohibition appropriate.

A similar situation obtains with respect to v. 28. Whether originally this saying was genuinely legal or simply moral admonition, any society in which adultery contravenes established mores can produce multiple settings in which it would be thoroughly intelligible without the antithetical formulation. That v. 28 is harmoniously situated in its present location following v. 27 is obvious. It simply is far from clear that this setting is required for the saying to communicate its meaning.

The idea that thesis and antithesis in the so-called primary forms are inseparable units of meaning is an overstatement of the case. If in fact Matthew created the third, fifth, and sixth antitheses, the argument from intelligibility does not constitute sufficient grounds for denying his responsibility for the first, second, and fourth, as well.

The above argument would appear to be adequate, if the antitheses all exhibited a form as simple as that at 5:31–32. However, to the simple antitheses "additional" material which appears once to have circulated as independent sayings has sometimes been attached. In the cases of the fifth and sixth antitheses the addenda are easily explained, if the Q hypothesis is regarded as valid. The apparent additions to the so-called primary antitheses, on the other hand, introduce a different problem. Paul Hoffmann, among others, regards them as evidence of the reworking of a more pristine, pre-Matthean form: "They too bear signs of having been worked over. In the first and second antitheses individual sayings were added on: 5:23f., 25f. (par. Luke 12:57–59 = Q); 5:29f. (par. Mark 9:43–48); the fourth antithesis was most probably expanded by the addition of 5:34b–36."[14]

Whether vv. 34b–36 represent an intrusion is so problematic that a decision with respect to it would obviously depend on the resolution of the other cases; it can be set aside. What must be shown in each instance is not merely that independent sayings have been added to the saying in the *antithesis proper,* since that could be accounted for in a number of ways. What must be shown is that the "primary" antithetical formulations have attracted extraneous material which seriously interferes with the structural pattern. For example, the Lord's Prayer seems to distort an inherited threefold section on almsgiving, prayer, and fasting in Matthew 6. A similar distortion of a received set of antithetically expressed rules might be taken as a sign of redactional alteration of the form.

In the complex Matt. 5:27–30 the final two verses clearly existed as independent sayings. V. 29 can be explained rather easily at whatever stage it was attached to v. 28; the "offending eye" is not offensively intrusive whether Matthew added it to a transmitted antithesis or incorporated it in a form he created. The hyperbole about cutting off a hand in v. 30 does not fit the context as smoothly, and it has been urged that v. 30 is jarringly out of place. The fact that the sayings in vv. 29–30 can be shown to have circulated together (Mark 9:43–48; Matt. 18:8–9) somewhat reduces the force of this judgment. Further, the association of both eyes and hands with the arousal of desire in rabbinic discussions of lust makes the content of v. 30 comprehensible.[15] Neither v. 29 nor v. 30 is inappropriately related to the subject matter of the second antithesis. The criterion of suitability to context is not irrelevant, since the hypothesis of the existence of a simple antithetical formulation without attached instruction is attested only for the manifestly secondary 5:31–32. Since in five cases there are appended sayings which appear to develop the significance of the antitheses, the idea that such sayings are intrusions inappropriate to the form is a doubtful assumption. Like vv. 34b–37, vv. 29–30 need not be understood as the evangelist's clumsy alteration of a received form.

The issue finally must be decided in relation to the first antithesis. Vv. 23–24, 25–26 are independent sayings whose presence at this point is infelicitous. What do such sayings have to do with an antithesis dealing with murder and anger? That question exists for us. The infelicity apparently was not recognized by the evangelist. And, because for him the love command is the law's succinct expression, the addition of positive instruction about reconciliation to a prohibition of anger is not inexplicable on either alternative open to us: namely, that vv. 21–22 (or 22a) reached him in his tradition or that the tradition in v. 22 was the "stuff" out of which he created the first antithesis. Moreover, on the assumption that the first antithesis is pre-Matthean, the problem of agglutination reaches back further than v. 23. Hoffmann, for example, by striking vv. 34b–36 from the fourth antithesis and vv. 29–30 from the second, arrives at an antithesis form with which the three-membered saying of v. 22 is formally out of balance. That is, vv. 21–22a correspond to vv. 27–28; but v. 22bc is excess baggage. Hoffmann is thoroughly consistent and does not shrink from this conclusion: the clauses in v. 22bc are "additions" made to render the prohibition of anger "practicable" for the church.[16] It is possible that v. 22b is a very early gloss; but the total dismemberment of v. 22 entails the rejection of a structural parallelism which seems arbitrary. The willingness to dispose of v. 22bc in this manner appears to me to result from the prior conclusion that, in some way, v. 22 can only be intelligible in an antithetical construct; once it is recognized that v. 22 can be understood independently, the parallel structure speaks against the proposed dismemberment. In fact, attributing the "additions" of v. 22 to the ecclesiastical concerns of the evangelist points up the thread which unites vv. 22–26. Without v. 21, the remaining sayings of the first antithesis belong together in the Matthean community as a series related to the life of the church; this is no less true of v. 22a than it is of 22c. "You shall not kill" in v. 21 has been set over against a prohibition of anger positively interpreted as a call to reconciliation. Matthew has supplied v. 21 as a fresh context for the once independent v. 22a(b)c.

If the so-called primary antitheses are not self-evidently pre-Matthean, the case cannot be regarded as closed in favor of the evangelist's responsibility for the form. The awkward strong adversative with which Luke 6:27 is introduced has been interpreted as evidence that something like the antithesis of Matt. 5:43–44 was to be found in Q. To W. D. Davies "Luke 6:27 suggests that the antitheses of Matthew 5 . . . had their parallel in a source behind Q: the verse 'But I say to you that hear . . . ' naturally implies a contrast, although it is unexpressed."[17] One must respond to this that, since the contrast is unexpressed, no real ground has been laid for demonstrating a primitive antithesis; there is a distinction between a *contrast* which might be introduced by "but" and an *antithesis* in the style of Matthew 5. The synoptics yield several examples of sayings which have admonitory, if not legal, tone and in which a contrast is expressed by means of "but." The nearest at hand is *within a Matthean antithesis:* "But I say to you, do not resist one who is evil, 'but' to him who strikes you on the right cheek, turn the other also" (5:39). Yet, that example illustrates what the normal expectation would be, namely, that the "but" clause would be preceded by a prohibition or negative assertion. Luke's "but," if taken over from Q, probably did not stand at the turning point of an antithesis. Of course, one should not engage in universal negatives, as my earlier treatment of this subject did by brushing Luke 6:27a aside quickly because of the absence of a negative statement in advance of the "but." Such aberrations are found. But would this explanation occur to anyone without a synopsis in which Matt. 5:43–44 was directly across the page? Probably not. And some other explanation seems to be called for.

Victor Furnish has recently joined those who see "the adversative construction [in Luke 6:27 as] . . . related to the preceding 'woes'."[18] By suggesting that the woes are "in effect prohibited actions," Furnish seeks to overcome the problem of the missing negative contrast which the "but" implies. Lagrange, on the other hand, thought that "Verse 27 would connect better to v. 23; after having said that the disciples would be hated, Jesus taught them to love their enemies; the context would be excellent."[19]

These attempts to explain Luke 6:27a share a common assumption: that 6:27a is the introduction to v. 27b as such. If that assumption is correct, then Lagrange's solution is probably the most satisfactory. However, if the assumption is mistaken and v. 27a has another relation to its context, then it is possible that Luke's awkward adversative is a red herring in the discussion of the antitheses. Another alternative, here stated with unintended dogmatism for the sake of brevity, is that Luke 6:27a was never meant as an introduction to v. 27b. Instead, it is a theme-bearing transition to the body of an exquisite homily, first organized in Q and edited by Luke without serious impairment of its structure. The outline of the homily would look something like the following:

6:20–26	Blessed are the poor . . .
	those who hunger now . . .
	those who weep now . . .
	Blessed are you when they hate you . . .
	[But woe . . .]
6:27a	But I say to you that hear . . .
6:27b–45	Love your enemies . . .
	And judge not . . .
	For (there is) no good tree . . .
6:46	Why do you call me 'Lord, Lord,' and do not what I tell you?
6:47–49	Everyone who comes . . . and hears my words
	and does them . . . but he who hears and does not do them.

As its concluding parabolic paragraph (vv. 47–49) tells us plainly, the purpose of the homily is to inculcate *hearing* and *doing* the *words* of Jesus. The body of this short sermon is a collection of these words (vv. 27b–45). There are two points of transition between the elements of the homily: v. 46, which thematically emphasizes *doing* what Jesus says; and v. 27a, which invites the audience to *hear* his words.[20] That is, Luke 6:27a introduces vv. 27b–45, not merely v. 27b. That does not remove the problem of the "but," but it is no longer the same problem. It simply has nothing to do with Matthew's or any other's antitheses and should be disregarded in that connection.

Thus, there appear to me no grounds which justify the notion that Matthew received the antithesis form in his tradition of the sayings of Jesus. The form is his own. By it he intends to assert the authority of Jesus' representation of the law over against what he alleges is Pharisaic interpretation of the law; he intends to set forth exemplary statements of the true Torah in obedience to which Christians practice the righteousness which exceeds that of the scribes and Pharisees. It does not matter whether Matthew accurately represents Pharisaic halakah; the section is too polemic to expect that such would be the case.[21] However inaccurate about or unfair to his opponents he may be, Matthew means the "But I say to you" of the antitheses to set law against law—the authoritative pronouncement of Jesus (the embodiment of Wisdom-Torah) against the misconstructions and misunderstandings of Torah among Matthew's adversaries.

It is because this intention is so clear that the numerous close approximations to the form frequently proposed fall just short of being finally convincing. It is not only that the rabbinic examples are not quite truly parallel; it is, rather, that the Matthean antithesis has lost its patience with scholarly debate and hurls forth the true Torah as incontrovertible pronouncement.

Nevertheless, one must remember that Matthew is not always impatient with legal debates. I am prepared to retreat from the position that the antitheses have no relation at all to rabbinic forms. A direct relation—a rabbinic form which Matthew copied in chap. 5—does not seem possible. But several of the suggested approximations are such that they might have been christologically transformed into the Matthean formula.

Whatever else is said about the "But I say to you" of the antitheses, it functions as an introductory formula to a legal ruling. The "I say" introduction formula in Matthew 5 has a different function, then, than "I say" and "Truly I say" sayings we usually find elsewhere.[22] Perhaps the closest thing to it in the New Testament are a few Pauline passages (notably in 1 Corinthians 7) where the apostle employs "I say" to introduce sentences in which rulings of a halakic character may be involved, but these cases are not antithetical.

Of course, the nearest parallel to the Matthew 5 construction is found in a context of legal debate in Matthew 19. The Matthean version of the dialogue concerning divorce culminates in vv. 8–9: "Moses . . . permitted you to divorce your wives . . . And I say to you, 'Whoever divorces his wife . . . and marries another commits adultery'." The form is particularly close to several examples of rabbinic debate cited by Smith[23] which exhibit the form "Rabbi So-and-so used to say . . . , but I say . . . " Yet, since Moses is *not* Rabbi So-and-so, and even without the imperious "I", there is something new in Matt. 19:8–9. What is new, how-

ever, is not so much formal as it is dogmatic; the content, more
than the structure, has been christologically transformed. Matt.
19:8–9 represents a kind of halfway house between Smith's rabbinic form and the antitheses of Matthew 5. It is only a halfway
house because in 19:3–9 academic dialogue is tolerated (i.e., vv.
8–9 complete and are integral to the debate as the evangelist constructed it); Matthew 5 issues pronouncements which are impatient with debate. Yet, it is fully a halfway house because v. 9,
though contrasted with what Matthew regarded as a concession, is
also set in contrast with Moses.[24] The distance from "Moses permitted . . . but I say" to "It was said . . . but *I* say" is a short
step. Yet, it is a significant step, for it completes the move from
scholarly dialectic to authoritative pronouncement. The antitheses
perhaps are not *de novo* creations. Their newness may be essen-
tially the dimension added and the setting altered by Matthew's
Christology.

In this connection, mention must be made of the appeal by
Jeremias to the criterion of dissimilarity in order to claim the
antithetical formulation for the historical Jesus.[25] Quite apart from
the opinion just expressed that the form in Matthew 5 may have
been adapted from an anterior rabbinic form by way of the development in Matt. 19:8–9, it is questionable whether the absence
of precise parallels to the antitheses in Judaism and early Christianity can be used in this way. Dissimilarity—the identification of
elements distinctively characteristic of a speaker or author—is as
valid for determining genuine Matthean material as it is for determining authentic Jesus tradition. The precise form found in
Matthew 5 does not appear in Judaism, elsewhere in early Christian documents, *or in other parts of the tradition about Jesus.* It
appears in one place only: immediately following Matt. 5:20 as
part of a systematic exposition of the righteousness exceeding that
of the Pharisees. To deny it to Matthew on the grounds of dissimilarity is to assume that the form is too bold for the evangelist
as an author. The whole sweep of the Sermon on the Mount is
itself too bold for such an assumption.

The authoritative declarations of chap. 5 rest firmly on Matthew's Christology. His programmatic challenge to Pharisaic

righteousness depends on his recognition of Jesus as the very embodiment of the Torah. His "But I say to you" does not set either the evangelist or the Lord he confesses in opposition to the Torah. He does not really intend to do any of those things we have traditionally associated with the antitheses: to abrogate the law "in principle," to proclaim a "new law," to deepen and spiritualize the law, and the like. Objectively, as outsiders to the Matthean context, we may be able to judge that the evangelist has in effect done some of these things. But this was not his purpose: his purpose was to define and exhibit the True Law and to call men to obedience to it as the first stage of discipleship.

not Jesus self-understanding

but

Matthew's understanding of Jesus as Lord

NOTES

1. M. J. Suggs, *Wisdom, Christology and Law in Matthew's Gospel* (Cambridge, Mass., 1970), 109–15.

2. D. Daube, *The New Testament and Rabbinic Judaism* (London, 1956), 55–60, 67–71.

3. Suggs, *Wisdom,* 109–15.

4. The position has been perceptively criticized by M. D. Johnson, "Reflections on a Wisdom Approach to Matthew's Gospel." *CBQ* 36 (1974), 44–64. The force of the critique is partially vitiated by a failure to recognize subtle distinctions between my position and that of Bultmann.

5. Eduard Schweizer, *Jesus* (Richmond, 1971), 31. The quotation is chosen as typical within a broad spectrum of opinion. Cf. G. Bornkamm, *Jesus of Nazareth* (New York, 1960), 103. Schweizer's careful definition of his position on the antitheses is now to be found in *Good News According to Matthew* (Atlanta, 1975), 110–17.

6. E.g., J. W. Bowman and R. W. Trapp, *The Gospel from the Mount* (Philadelphia, 1957), 58.

7. L. E. Keck, "The Sermon on the Mount," in D. G. Miller and D. Y. Hadidian (eds.), *Jesus and Man's Hope* (Pittsburgh, 1970) II, 319.

8. R. Bultmann, *The History of the Synoptic Tradition* (New York/Evanston, ²1968), 135–36.

9. "Die bessere Gerechtigkeit," *BibLeb* 10 (1969), 180; the first ellipsis conceals significant qualifications made by Hoffmann which will be examined below.

10. On v. 22 cf. K. Stendahl, "Matthew," in M. Black and H. H. Rowley (eds.), *Peake's Commentary on the Bible* (New York, 1962), 776: "In the light of the disciplinary rules from Qumran with their high ideals of brotherhood within the community we must raise the question with new seriousness whether the ethical concern here is intramural . . . Such an interpretation has much to commend it, especially since the relation between cultic action and the mutual forgiveness of the brethren is a strong motif in Mt. (see 6:14; 18:15–20) . . ."

11. C. G. Montefiore, *The Synoptic Gospels* (London, 1909), II: 58.

12. G. Strecker, *Der Weg der Gerechtigkeit* (FRLANT 82; Göttingen, ³1971), 133, regards the passage in James as independent of Matthew but he still treats vv. 33–37 as pre-Matthean as a whole. The thesis is retained because it is the form of a prohibition.

13. Bultmann, *History,* 91; see also the brief note in the Supplement, 395.

14. "Gerechtigkeit," 180.

15. See Strack-Billerbeck I: 299–301; C. G. Montefiore, *Rabbinic Literature and Gospel Teachings* (London, 1930), 41.

16. "Gerechtigkeit," 184.

17. W. D. Davies, *The Setting of the Sermon on the Mount* (Cambridge, 1964), 388. Davies regards the "but" as a vestigial trace of an antithetical form.

18. *The Love Commandment in the New Testament* (Nashville, 1972), 55.

19. M. R. Lagrange, *Évangile selon saint Luc* (Paris, 1948), 192, cited by J. Dupont, *Les Béatitudes I, Le problème littéraire* (Paris, 1969), 315; see Dupont, *Béatitudes,* 189–96, 312–21.

20. The parallel at Mark 3:7–12 suggests that Luke 6:17 has been influenced by the homily; but see Dupont, *Béatitudes,* 189–90. P. S. Minear, "Jesus' Audiences, according to Luke," *NovTest* 16 (1974), 105–08, also understands Luke 6:27a as introducing "a whole block of teaching"; in his view, it marks a change in audience from the "disciples" in vv. 20–26 to the "crowds" in vv. 27b–49. (My colleague W. R. Baird, Jr. brought this article to my attention.)

21. Matt. 6:1–18, which is still controlled by the polemic concern to commend a better righteousness than that of Pharisaic practice, implies that the "hypocrites" (= the Pharisees) never engaged in an unostentatious piety—which contradicts what we know to have been the case. In polemic, one may be very careful to state his own position accurately, but opponents are often caricatured.

22. The most frequent use of "I say" in formulaic phrases is

the solemn asseverative introduction ("I say to you"; "Truly I say to you"). As such it introduces a wide variety of forms: eschatological judgment sentences, wisdom-apocalyptic revelations, sayings, admonitions, words of commendation/condemnation.

23. M. Smith, *Tannaitic Parallels to the Gospels* (JBLMS 6; Philadelphia, 1951), 27–30.

24. See D. Daube, "Concessions to Sinfulness in Jewish Law," *JJS* 10 (1959), 1–13.

25. J. Jeremias, *New Testament Theology* I (New York, 1971), 251.